DESERT WAR DIARY

First edition, published in 2000 by

WOODFIELD PUBLISHING
Woodfield House, Babsham Lane, Bognor Regis
West Sussex PO21 5EL, England.

ISBN 1-873203-59-4

Desert War Diary

Memories of 213 Squadron 1941-1945

JOHN G. WALTON

Woodfield Publishing
~ WEST SUSSEX • ENGLAND ~

Hurricanes of 213 Squadron in the Western Desert, 1942.

Dedicated to the memory
of all the men who served with 213 Squadron
both on the ground and in the air
during World War Two

IRRATATUS LACESSIT CRABRO

"THE HORNET ATTACKS WHEN ROUSED"

'Such is life and life is such,
And after all it isn't much.
First a candle then a hearse,
It might have been better,
But it could have been worse.'

Norman Wisdom

Contents

The author, taken in Cairo, 1942.

PART ONE

Exploits in Convoy

THURSDAY 22ND MAY, 1941

Left Greenock on Thursday night at 8.30pm and proceeded through the upper part of Irish Sea into the Atlantic Ocean, then west towards America. Only two days from the coast we change our course to avoid packs of German submarines, let's hope for the best. On our journey we sleep near the bottom of the boat and can hear the waves banging against the side of the ship, wave after wave, it's quite frightening for us non-sailors. We sleep on mattresses or hammocks, if you have the privilege of being first you get a mattress, second, a hammock!

SATURDAY 24TH MAY

Somewhere out in the Atlantic Ocean at 10.15am we are alerted for 'boat stations' with lifejackets strapped around us in case of emergency. I must say there is quite a panic. A German bomber (a JU88) was after the convoy, but fortunately we have an aircraft carrier with us and some of its planes took off and brought the JU down, with the help of the cruiser *Exeter* – three cheers!

TUESDAY 22ND MAY

Causing great anxiety for our convoy, the aircraft carrier *Argus*, with Fairey Fulmars on board, was alerted about German warship proceeding towards us. This caused more than a little bit of panic because it was believed to be one of Germany's biggest warships. Thank God everything's calmed down because there's no place to run out here like there is on dry land. One torpedo and we would all be blown to pieces! Fortunately, we are still here, but there goes the aircraft carrier on its way to the Med, now that all-clear has been called.

WEDNESDAY 28TH MAY

We are part of the biggest ever going to the Middle East – over 200 troopships. We are zig-zagging because of German U-boats and cannot risk going through Gibraltar; we have to go all the way down and around the horn of Africa. I hope it's no worse than the rough passage through the Bay of Biscay.

THURSDAY 29TH MAY

We have just got out of the Bay of Biscay (hell, what next? I have been sick for two days). In the early hours of the morning there was a panic. We strapped on lifejackets and were on emergency stand-by for six hours following an announcement over our tannoy. *Zulu*, *Kosic* and *Exeter* were sent out to attack Germany's biggest warship, the *Bismark*. Seemingly there was quite a battle which made its way out into the Atlantic Ocean. Fortunately they were joined by another aircraft carrier, not attached to our convoy. Its Fairey Swordfish gave the *Bismark* such a pasting with their torpedoes that the Germans aboard scuttled her and were taken prisoners. Thank God our lads sunk it before it reached our convoy – its gun range was 20 miles! We can stand down now and be on our way. I intend to get my head down – I'm whacked!

SUNDAY 1ST JUNE, 1941

Three days off the Equator and more surprises. Two long distance flying boats (Dorniers) dropped bombs on our convoy. Two troopships were damaged but not badly, thank the Lord, but the German flying boats had an unhappy ending. Then we had to stand-by and strap up for another emergency, lifejackets and boat stations in case something went wrong. We stood on deck for two hours before the all-clear came through. Apparently three German submarines were circling our convoy, but they did not attack. I guess our warships were a bit too much for them when they started dropping depth charges and carrying out strategic manoeuvres, trying to fool the subs by shooting flares into the sky. It's very hard to adapt to these emergencies. One never knows what's coming next – maybe 'Davey Jones's Locker' at the bottom of the Atlantic Ocean!

MONDAY 2ND – THURSDAY 5TH JUNE

We arrived at the equator in the afternoon, and there was a ceremony with the barber and 'King Neptune' performing their rites with a big wooden razor. Competitors were knocked off a pole into a makeshift swimming pool and then shaved by a whitewash brush for a certificate of passing over the equator. I never participated, it seemed a bit much for me!

FRIDAY 6TH JUNE

We are proceeding into our first port of call for water and food, etc, looking onto land about a mile or maybe a little more. Then all these 'bum boats' advanced towards our ship, natives coming out with their bargains of bananas, coconuts, grapes and what have you. They're shouting for us to throw a silver coin into the sea and "we dive for it". Believe it or not they bring the coins up in their mouths. Looking towards land we could see Freetown, Sierra Leone, which didn't impress me any. We expect to move out early morning; we aren't allowed off boat.

SATURDAY 7TH JUNE

Little did we know that the Germans occupied the port a little to the north of Freetown, at a place called Dakar. Fortunately we had plenty of air support, flying boats (Sunderland's). Any sighting of U-boats and they would signal to our warships. However, we are well out into the Atlantic Ocean without a hitch proceeding down towards Gulf-of Guinea. I often look across towards the horizon, longing for home, with the thought in the back of my mind that I might never have the opportunity to return. What could be nicer? With my hopes of marriage and to settle down. Better than any glory or medals. Oh dear, there goes the alarm for stand-by boats again. Strap up with lifejacket. I only hope it works should I need it!

Eighteen German aircraft (Dornier flying boats) were on reconnaissance over our convoy, but thank God the all clear is sounded. It certainly makes you uncomfortable...

MONDAY 9TH JUNE

We proceed on to the Gulf of Guinea and have to start zip-zagging again to throw off any U-boat packs, which are very active around these parts, especially with a convoy of over 200 ships, the biggest so far that's attempted to go around Africa and up the Red Sea. There goes the alarm for boat stations again. An hour goes by before the all-clear. Surprises every day, but never good ones!

TUESDAY 10TH TO THURSDAY 19TH JUNE

For 11 days the procedure is much the same. Wide open spaces of nothing but sea and more zig-zagging with the convoy trying to avoid U-boats. There were one or two German flying boats doing a check on our convoy, reconnaissance without success, and the guns on our warships put a sting in their tails according to ship's noticeboard. We are on our way around Cape Town, then our port of call will be Durban, South Africa. I can't wait, because we are allowed ashore. What a relief after all these weeks at sea. I wonder what it's like on dry land?

FRIDAY 20TH JUNE

Arrived at Durban, South Africa, at 5.30pm. No shore leave today because of stand-by duty on *Georgic* for 24 hours. What a night at the dockside! Taxis tooting, brass bands going full blast, ships by the dozen all lit up – you would hardly think there was a war going on – lights all over the place. It just seems like a dream, and a far cry from leaving Greenock with nothing but the blackout. The lads who were first to go ashore had a good welcome with the voice of The White Lady over the tannoy, singing beautifully and saying the taxis will take you anywhere in Durban.

SATURDAY 21ST JUNE

Dry land at last! For the first time since 22nd May. When I came down the gangway I bent down and kissed the dock floor, what a sentimental feeling! You have got to be here to experience it. We were escorted to a Scottish church with tables full of all sorts of food and drink, everything you could mention. I met a Navy lad from Chester-le-Street, and after the meal we went for a trip on a rickshaw and then dropped off at picture house, all free. Jim Lee went to his ship and I to mine at 11.10 pm after an enjoyable evening. What nice people!

SUNDAY 22ND JUNE

We were invited back to the Scottish Church canteen with tables again full of whatever you wanted. Jim Lee and I met Mr and Mrs Wilson, and after our meal they took us to see Zulu-land and its warriors. After that performance we were taken back to their farm, which was like a ranch, for tea and supper. What a real good day and what a way to end our stay. Arrangements were made for us to go back next day, as unfortunately we were moving out after the parade through the streets of Durban, back to the *Georgic*. What fantastic people! It really is sad to hear the bands playing and the White Lady singing as we pull away from the docks. I cry to think that these people we are leaving have no thoughts of killing and yet the whole purpose of our convoy is to do just that. What a bloody world! And politicians cause quite a lot of it. Power and money are definitely the root of all evil.

I reckon that rat's sleep better than we do on the *Georgic*. We are right down in the bottom of the ship and always fighting for a place. Many's the time I can't get a mattress or a hammock and have to sleep on the bare floor. Meanwhile the bloody officers sleep in their white sheets and have parties above deck (it's true) – talk about different places for the rich and poor! – I reckon we would be better off as POWs while our officers are on a cruise – they've even got nurses on the same deck! There are signs up on deck sating "Officers Only". It makes me sick and I say it stinks – after all, we're all human and we are fighting for the same thing and yet all the lads are treated as lower class. Still, we have to keep our chins up and carry on with our duties!

FRIDAY 27TH JUNE

Still heading miles and miles out into the Indian Ocean. Calmer seas now, almost as though you could walk on the water. We are ploughing away up towards Gulf of Aden. One of our cruisers, *HMS Exeter*, catapulted a Walrus aircraft to go on reconnaissance; unfortunately they were missing for quite a while. At 5.20pm we got word that it crashed into the sea and all they found was one body with only head and shoulders; they never found the other three. The next day the convoy flew flags at half-mast and we had a burial at sea for the airman, on Saturday 28th June, 1941. I must say it was very emotional with all of us thinking that we may be next.

We called in at Aden for supplies, only stayed for a few hours, nobody allowed off ship, then proceeded into the Red Sea. You would think we were on a glass surface, I've never seen any sea as calm and we've come through quite a few.

I almost forgot to mention the food, which is fairly good and we are well catered for especially on the mess deck. Very good except when storms brew up. I must admit missing a few meals through seasickness. Believe me if the ship sank I couldn't have cared less, I was so sick, an awful feeling I wouldn't wish on my worst enemy. The worst was the Bay of Biscay, it was a nightmare! But when things calm down its not so bad, and at night, the sea can be like a fairground with illuminations, movements and reflections of various species of fish – spectacular beyond imagination.

SUNDAY 29TH JUNE

We have a few thousand miles to go. We are going up the Red Sea and German aircraft are within range from their desert aerodromes. Hopefully, our air support can cope with them. The *Georgic* has the largest number of troops, Army, Navy and Airforce, and the Germans have tried very hard indeed to seek an opportunity to sink it.

We are now making towards Port Sudan and all we can see from our ship is sand and, now and again, palm trees, very few, but nice to see, also traders with their camels. We seem to just cruise off the coast of West Africa, all the way until the Gulf of Suez.

TUESDAY 8TH JULY

We have reached our disembarkation port, Port Tewfick. We stay here a couple of days in tents, until all of our equipment is unloaded from the ship. Lorries, food, water, etc for our journey to Kasafreet, that's the pool place for all troops in Middle East from England. Two of our transport drivers who have been back and forward from the ship, have just told us the *Georgic* has been bombed by a Junkers 88 with quite a few killed. Fancy coming all this way and being killed, it doesn't seem fair somehow.

THURSDAY 10TH JULY

The bombing of the ship happened at approximately 8.30am. Fortunately, the RAF were first to disembark so we were very lucky. They say damage to the ship is considerable and it will be out of action for a long time.

We arrived at our land destination, Kasafreet. Probably we will spend a few weeks here to recuperate from our long sea voyage – almost three months. There's no chance of running away, we are surrounded by nothing but miles and miles of sand – maybe it's for the best... During the day IT'S HOT! You could almost fry an egg on the sand, but at night from 10pm until dawn it's really very cold. I'm sleeping with all my clothes on, my overcoat on top then my ground sheet, even though we are in tents.

What a place! We have to make sure everything that's valuable, even clothes, are put into a kit bag and used for a pillow, with a brass ring and lock around the top of bag. These Arabs would even nick your drawers while you were sleeping! Fortunately we have the RAF Regiment on guard, which is a blessing, you can't be too careful. The Arab kids are worse than their elders. I always keep a tight hold of my wallet and pay book. They know that if they nick a pay book they will be in the money. Fagin has got nothing on this lot!

I keep mine between my vest and shoulder with string around the neck all the time. It's a golden rule, look after your paybook, or maybe have a long stay in jail!

FRIDAY 11TH JULY

We are still waiting to re-form our squadron, No. 213 (Hurricanes). We have to dig trenches near our tents because of air raids. Italian aircraft visit our camp day and night, dropping flares and bombs and strafing. Some of the bombs have all sorts inside them: nails, bits of steel and welded stars made of shrapnel. It's terrifying hearing them flying over our trenches, sometimes sleep is impossible. I think the Italian aircraft come from the desert in Libya. Let's hope for a bit of sleep tonight!. What a lovely sunset, maybe that's a sign to settle in. I'm in bed by 10 o'clock, groundsheet for my bed, a peaceful night, thank God.

SATURDAY 12TH JULY

Early morning breakfast was half-an-hour late, it should have been 6.30am. We take it easy in the afternoon because it's far too hot for working, that's why we rise early, when it's nice and cool. There are millions of flies biting all the time, what a bloody nuisance, and young Arab kids, pestering to flog their eggs and fruit, bartering for cigarettes, it's hard to tell which is worse! Then there's the heat, sand flies and mosquitoes. It's quite a laugh before going to bed, rigging up your bed then your mosquito net, and, of course, there are the scorpions too. A DIY system has to be put into use, making some sort of raised bed, I used stones, anything to avoid bites and stings.

I don't suppose our squadron will be formed until a confirmed destination is marked out, maybe another few weeks or more.

Looking up into the beautiful moonlight, I'm thinking that the same moon will be shining over home and wondering what my beloved ones are doing at this time, 11.30pm. I can feel the cold creeping in, it's almost same temperature as winter in England all through the night.

SUNDAY 13TH / MONDAY 14TH JULY

We moved to a new campsite not far from Isamlia, still waiting for aircraft and equipment, what a place! We pitched our tents and our Adjutant gave a speech, I think it was to keep us from being bored, about living conditions and protection from heat and how the natives would take the pillow from under your head when you were sleeping and you'd never know it was gone. Isamlia is not too far from camp, only you have to be very careful walking through lanes of sugar cane which are near the camp – you can almost smell the wogs in there.

TUESDAY 15TH JULY

The Adjutant put the squadron to work digging trenches, as we still get visitors at night, Italian planes, which definitely raise merry hell, even though we have no aircraft yet, and to make it more uncomfortable they drop flares and the whole place lights up. We have a bit of a NAAFI canteen. I think I'll go and get one or two items before the Ities come over again. I hope for a little sleep tonight, which is difficult with one eye open for 'wogs' breaking into your tent and the other watching for flares. It was never like this at home!

WEDNESDAY 16TH JULY

We are still digging trenches. They are a boon to our safety, as one never knows what those Italians are up to. We get quite a few visits through day, but the aircraft are well up into those blue skies, too scared to come down any lower. Our hands are blistering and very sensitive, but we soldier on for better or for worse. This working hard certainly boosts morale, and we play a bit of football.

THURSDAY 17TH JULY

This waiting to form this 213 Squadron seems to be a bit of a drag, but our Adjutant insists on giving us plenty to do, not letting our minds stray. It's really hard to find any entertainment like we have in England, but we do our best. We have a lorry taking us into Isamlia. I have my photograph taken to send home. It takes an hour or so to develop, but when I call back for them they are very good, Robert Taylor hasn't a look in! We went into picture house after that and enjoyed it very much, then back to camp at 11.30 and into bed by 11.45. It's hard to believe there's a war on, it is so peaceful at the moment in Isamlia. It is a beautiful night.

FRIDAY 18TH JULY

This horrible heat and the flies! We have sandstorms too. We go to the cookhouse where our meals are served, but before we get there our plates are covered with sand. I usually carry a big paper bag to stop the sand getting onto the plate. Then we proceed to one of the meals tents, we have outside tent mesh traps for flies. They work well and are full before you can say "Jack Robinson". We also carry the old fly swatter What have I done to deserve this - Germans, sandstorms, flies.

My bed at the moment is something I made myself, something like an ordinary camp bed, only the part I sleep on is two old sacks ripped in two and nailed to the cross-struts. We are not supplied with beds at the moment, perhaps some kind Jerry may help later!

SATURDAY 19TH JULY

More digging trenches. We must have dug half the bloody desert up! We start in the morning and finish at about noon because the heat here is unbearable in the afternoons. We park ourselves down until 6.30 or 7.00 when it slowly cools down.

To tell the truth I'm beginning to feel like one of these rats that run about in this desert, I grow more like one every day that passes and almost think, eat and breathe like one. Perhaps we may move soon, who knows. Patience is a virtue, so they say, but we are running short of it...

SUNDAY 20TH JULY – SATURDAY 2ND AUGUST

We are more or less getting the squadron together. 'C' Flight has been attached to 73 Squadron at Sidi Hanaish, and they have shot down four ME109s and a ME110 damaged. The remainder of the squadron flew convoy patrols before strafing enemy tanks and transport in the Bardia area. We of 213 Squadron are suddenly moved to Lydda, Palestine, where in company with Nos. 80 and 260 Squadrons, we take part in the Syrian campaign. Although a 'side-show', from the main desert campaign, No 213 has had a busy couple of weeks of ground attack work including raiding airfields at Messkine Takia, and Aleppo. One of the Hurricanes used during this period was W9290 AK-B. We have been kept busy re-arming guns and bombs. At last we have seen some action!

SUNDAY 3RD AUGUST

After an unsatisfactory first few months. Squadron Leader Lockhart, the new commanding officer, has finally assembled his squadron at LG90, near Amriya. The full squadron is here. These last few months we have been kicked around from pillar to post, so let's hope for a spell at Amriya until the end of December...

SUNDAY 10TH AUGUST

We had a parade at 6pm. We are on the move again We were told by our Squadron Commander not to tell what ship we will embark on or our port of call. All our kitbags are on their way already. We have to carry our tropical kitbags with us.

THURSDAY 14TH AUGUST

Embarked at Port Said on *HMS Abdiel*, destroyer, our destination, Cyprus. We board the ship late at night and the only place we can sleep is on deck, with all our equipment, including our back packs, water bottles, etc. Lucky the Mediterranean Sea is kind to us and we have a very smooth night on board the *Abdiel*. What a journey, sailors stepping over us, the deck is packed, we are like sardines in a tin. What a sitting target for the German or Italian planes.

FRIDAY 15TH AUGUST

What a way to spend my birthday, on a cruise in the Mediterranean, and to think that people before the war paid quite a lot of money for a holiday cruise. Mind you, our cruise is more exciting, looking for enemy aeroplanes and submarines and sweating with full pack, etc. It's impossible to sleep, the ship keeps changing course, zig-zagging, to put off German submarines. Thank the Lord we are still afloat after almost two days on this ship. We hope to arrive tomorrow morning, somewhere along the coast of Cyprus.

SATURDAY 16TH AUGUST

We are awakened by speakers at 2 o'clock in the morning. Arrived at Famagusta, Cyprus. My eyes are blurred, what a time to be disembarked then walked to a train. We see a train unlike any to be found in England with coaches made of wood, something like those you might find in a fairground at home and the rails are as narrow as I've ever seen in my whole life! I am dragging two kit bags, full kit on my body, I feel worn out and still half asleep. How much can we survive? We arrive in camp up a wadi near Nicosia, tents are available and we are in bed by 5pm and I sleep until next day. What a hell of a journey!

PART TWO

Cyprus

SUNDAY 17TH AUGUST

Our advance party built our armoury out of petrol drums with benches inside and a room for duty, so we are all hands to work. I cleaned guns and equipment ready for action on the Hurricanes. We eased off for the afternoon and transport was laid on for a swimming session at Kyrenia. A great day for us all, a lovely place, and we came back to the armoury to finish off, preparing our planes to go on sortie tomorrow. Finished work at 10pm, in bed by 11. We seem to be kept busy at all hours, no sleep for the wicked!

MONDAY 18TH AUGUST

Up at 6am on stand-by for any emergency. We reload guns and prepare to fit small bombs for sorties against transport and aerodromes in Turkey along the Aegean coast, which is occupied by the Germans. At the moment we ground crews are not allocated to any specific aeroplane yet, we just work on any aircraft. Part of our squadron is on loan for reconnaissance work over Lebanon and Syria and based at Lydda in Lebanon, just near the Syrian border, for a short spell, while the rest of the squadron is guarding Cyprus and flying patrols over the Dodecanese Islands and Rhodes. Our aircraft here in Cyprus have just returned from a sortie and had quite a score, apparently, strafing aeroplanes, workshops, trains and transport. All returned safely without bruises. There is talk about us moving into joining the desert squadrons but at the moment just faint whispers.

TUESDAY 19TH AUGUST

A busy day on the aerodrome with army sappers trying to make a good landing strip. At the moment it's hard as rock. Our pilots can only use part of it to take off and land. The sappers are trying to improve it so that they can land from North, South, East or West. They have made sand bag revetments to prevent aircraft being hit by shrapnel should we get visitors, which we do at odd times. Last night the 'Ities' came over and it was better than the illuminations at Blackpool, but with more fireworks! We watched from our trenches and had a few 'near misses' with shrapnel and tracers flying about over our heads. But we have a good aerodrome defence; our army lads have Bofors guns and kept the Ities well above our heads so they could not dive-bomb us.

WEDNESDAY 20TH AUGUST

I suppose we should consider ourselves lucky, there's a cinema in Nicosia only five miles down the road and we have a NAAFI where we can go to sup a beer or two, although its just a marquee surrounded by sand bags. I think I will go to the cinema tonight. Transport leaves at six and it's my night off after a good long spell. Quite a few English people live in Nicosia, but we've been told that they keep themselves to themselves.

Had a good session at the pictures and enjoyed every minute of it – a John Wayne cowboy film. Arrived back in camp by 11.30, tucked up and away with the angels.

Woke two hours later. Some bloody Itie is dropping bombs on us. No damage, so all's well and back to sleep.

THURSDAY 21ST AUGUST

I am duty armourer tonight, and this afternoon I'm stripping a .303 Browning and cleaning it, in case any guns in our aircraft have been damaged. Fortunately, no problems yet. I've worked all afternoon and I'm on schedule for rearming and fixing guns, with boxes of ammunition at the ready. I'll bed down and keep a rifle at my side. You can't trust the Turks who live here in Cyprus, they are very sensitive at the moment and I feel something will blow out of proportion one day between the Greek and Turkish Cypriots, you can almost feel the tension between them when you are out an about in Nicosia or eating out in one of the many small but efficiently run restaurants. They are always asking us if we have anything to sell, that is to say Army or RAF equipment of any type, for which they would pay a good price. Of course it is more than our lives are worth to do such a thing (literally, the penalty is death by firing squad). One chap from the Army was caught selling materials and was sent to

Alexandria, Egypt. We never heard any more about him, but no way would I want to be in his shoes!

After all that things started to tighten up around the aerodrome. They brought in the RAF Regiment along with the Army and also issued passes to everybody. What with the war outside and the tension between the Turks and Greeks, this place feels like a pile of explosives waiting for a spark to set the whole lot off. Let's hope we get off this island before things erupt.

FRIDAY 22ND AUGUST

They call this island 'the Jewel of the Mediterranean' because its so beautiful. At the moment its particularly important to Britain, given it's strategic position in the Mediterranean Sea. Its a pity to think that all this friction in Cyprus is caused by religion. I'm almost asleep, so I must give up, besides all I'm using for light is a small tin with a hole in the centre and a wick made out of string dipped in paraffin. If you don't improvise around here you just have to do without.

SATURDAY 23RD AUGUST

Up at 6.30am. Panic stations. Seven Hurricanes to be made ready for action arrived at Nicosia aerodrome. We check guns for ammunition slackness to provide easy firing and load small bombs, four on each wing, then stick the fuses in. All seems well. The sortie is to be over Crete, whatever they see they will just have a go at. Ready for take-off. I hope they all return and there are no snags. Then we're on our way back to the workshop, cleaning rifles and preparing for the duty armourer tonight. Whispers say that we may be moving to Ismailia and Idku, although not for a while yet.

We hear the drone of aircraft. Yes, all seven have returned, coming in to land, taxiing up to their bunkers. Two have been shot at, bullet holes in fuselage and tail, but according to our riggers they'll mend all right; all bombs gone and ammunition, without snags.

All aircraft will be ready for sorties tomorrow and fitted with long range petrol tanks under the wings. Should there be an emergency it's possible to release them to gain speed and manoeuvrability, until now we've had no mishaps. Pilots tell us 213 have scored well.

SUNDAY 24TH AUGUST

One of our aircraft is being fitted out for secret reconnaissance over a German base in Crete. I fit a camera, slotted into the wing, and there are two special long-range petrol tanks fitted by riggers, because it will take some time to get there. For the photographs, the pilot has to fly as low as possible, which definitely takes some doing. The pilot will use his emergency tanks on the way out, then release them.

He's been a long time over his target now and we are panicking a bit. We keep hearing noises of all kinds but no aircraft sounds. It's not surprising how attached we are to our pilots, what guts they have, knowing the risks they have to take. Suddenly there it is, our long-lost aircraft roaring in over the aerodrome minus its long range tanks.

It's taxiing towards our bunkers. I walk over to the aircraft, release the camera and take it to the photographer's workshop. We won't know results because of the secrecy; the film only goes to one person, Squadron Leader Lockhart. All we can get from the pilot is that he got some 'quite good' shots and there's not even a scratch on aircraft. When coming back he flew very low over the sea as the aircraft is well camouflaged from ME 109s. He had one or two scares, but made it home OK. That shows the skills of our flying lads; they are so very young but ready for battle in any part of the skies. That's my duties finished for today and I'm away to bed – 11.30pm – I'll sleep like a log!

MONDAY 25TH AUGUST

Well, what do you know? I have a day of freedom with some of the lads. We have the privilege of transport to Kyrenia, so we go swimming on a very good beach. It's quite a fantastic place, and we have a walk around the harbour, finding it very pleasant, especially the Cypriot people. Then we stroll into the country, about two miles and what do we find? An English house, with three elderly ladies running it as a garden cafe. There were tables placed around trees, the rich smell of all kinds of pastries and... coffee! Honestly, I thought we were back home, and the ladies couldn't do enough for us. As it was our first time there everything was free. Seemingly, they had been born out here and their family left them the house, so it was turned into a cafe especially for our troops. How nice to sit under a shade of trees for coffee and blackberry pie, also apple and rhubarb. What a lot of legends they told us, about various places on Cyprus, such as pagan shrines. Here, in antiquity, the Cypriot worshipped Zeus, the God of Hospitality; Aprhodite, the Goddess of Love and Beauty, also Artemis, Apollo, Dionysius Asclepios. The gods are still here on their sites and sanctuaries. Christians and Byzantines built churches which still adorn the countryside. Monasteries at Macheras, Kykko, Trooditissa, Chryssoroyiatissa, Ayios Neophytos, Holy Cross at Omodhos. Churches at Peristerona, 11th Century, Asinou, 1106 AD, Nikitari Saviour and BVM at Palechori, Panayia Tou Araka, Langoudhera, Archangelos and Podithou, Galata; Maria Theotokos and Ayios Nicholaos, 11th Century, Kakopetrios. Holy Cross, Pelendri and St. John, Lambadistis, Kalopanayiotis, Archangelos, Pedhoulas. All of these are very special to Cypriots; famous monasteries, e.g. Kykko Asino, Araka, containing impressive and well preserved, wonderful Byzantine frescoes and icons, real works of art. Those ladies have a great deal of knowledge about Cyprus and wrote all this out for me while we had tea. We stayed in the orchard four hours.

Then it was time to catch the transport back to camp. After I'd had a bit of supper I copied the notes from the ladies, finished at 12.30. I'm packing in now and away for some sleep.

TUESDAY 26TH AUGUST

Up at 6.30am. I wash and shave in my improvised basin, made from a petrol can. There are no means of bathing or showering here.

After breakfast I'm on way to the aerodrome at Nicosia. Three aircraft on sorties and I'm preparing to test guns, unload rounds from breach and test the button on the control column, and colours of the day, to fire when landing, also trigger for bombs all put back ready for service with guns loaded. And they're away off to Rhodes, to strafe and bomb important targets at Lindos, all with long-range tanks fitted under their wings. A second possible mission to small islands off Rhodes, Armogos and Astipala. There are rumours that German paratroops are ready for any emergency along the African coast, where the desert war is still going on. But Air Vice-Marshal Arthur Coningham and General Auchinlech have our forces well prepared for an invasion.

We are keeping our eyes open for our aircraft returning.

I must make a visit to 'Desert Lily' the dry toilet, dug out of the sand with boards around and hessian surrounds. What a pong! Plenty of flies too, so we have to take a swatter for protection!

Thank God! We see our aircraft returning. They taxi in, pilots get out, all ammo gone and bombs too. A successful operation with no mishaps, photos taken, will know tomorrow what the score was, unless it's very secret.

Now its time to re-arm and bomb up, ready for tomorrow's trip. 7am for first sortie.

WEDNESDAY 27TH AUGUST

Up early at 5am, ready for sorties. This time six aircraft will take off. Breakfast at 5.30am then off to the aerodrome. We just arrive there when flares are dropped from an enemy aircraft. But our 'planes are very well camouflaged with nets over the bunkers. Our sortie goes out a little later than scheduled, but better late than never. Three hours late, our aircraft take off on their way to a small island, Kos – their targets, heavy German weapons for invasion. This will be a tough island to crack. Every part of Kos is bristling with very powerful guns. Our planes will have to fly as low as possible; dive-bombing would be suicide for any pilot and a waste of an aircraft.

Fortunately, we haven't lost any planes yet, and all arrive back from Kos with empty fuel tanks, and all ammunition and bombs gone. Two planes have a few bullet holes, again, but no one hurt, and all aircraft safe, tucked away. Now they must be re-armed and bombed-up for tomorrow, 'colours of the day' added inside the pouch of the flare pistol. Working with battery lights we finish at 1.45am, in bed by 2am.

THURSDAY 28TH AUGUST

Up at 6.30am, off to the cookhouse, finish breakfast by 7am, then on by transport to the aerodrome. What a waste of time! The order to 'stand down' just came through from Operations. One thing about Cyprus we have good weather, although towards the end of the year apparently it can be as bad as England.

I'm enjoying sunbathing after last night's hard work. Then the siren's buzzing, and we jump into trenches. Two Messerschmitt 109Es have been spotted bearing down on us. The army guns give them hell. We are heavily defended by well-equipped artillery. They must have been reconnaissance planes that thought we were an easy target. They must have been very surprised indeed, they scarpered like lightning!

No sorties for 213 Squadron today so we are all back to our wigwams (tents). I went to the Naafi and bought two bottles of beer and some biscuits, took them back to my tent and drank myself to sleep.

FRIDAY 29TH AUGUST

God knows why I'm writing this memo. Why the hell are we here? The way news comes across the radio, we are fighting for a better life and for our future, but if you ask me, history never changes; everything will be the same as before. But, soldier on Jack! No rest for the wicked! At least writing this gives me something to do, especially as there's little we can do for entertainment on camp. Roll on Blighty and bugger this war! I'm sick to death of these cock-and-bull stories of Churchill and Montgomery and all the top brass and politicians telling us we are fighting for a better future. Isn't that what they said in the First World War? And look at all the people out of work, hardly surviving on what they're supposed to live on. Poverty everywhere. What a waste of everything that's meant to be for the good! Will we be worse off in 20 or 30 years' time, like in 1936 with strikes and blackshirts? I wonder...

I've had two easy days, and caught up on my correspondence. All seems very quiet at the moment. What a bloody war!

SATURDAY 30TH / SUNDAY 31ST AUGUST

We have been working on Nicosia aerodrome armoury, we have a big inspection in 30 hours on .303 Brownings, so we strip, pull-through, oil and grease, put them back into the aircraft and test for firing before re-arming. Everything OK, now to re-arm. There are times when all ground crew and armourers must be on alert. That's why we've been on the aerodrome these past two days. Something's going on, but we don't know what. That's the way it happens out here, nothing to do and then everything is 'go go go' non-stop. I sometimes feel our pilots are a bit crazy for wanting to see action all the time rather than just occasionally. That also goes for Squadron Leader Lockhart.

After two days preparing for action, we have to stand down. Squadron Leader Lockhart gives us a 'talk' explaining the stand down. It seems something big is happening on the German side; they're moving equipment from important islands to certain parts of Africa for some big push, when, we don't know, but it looks as if it won't be long before there's a big bang and our squadron will be stuck here on Cyprus and miss the show. The whole squadron seems a bit browned off at the prospect. Anyway, we are sleeping in the armoury on the aerodrome tonight just in case of a panic. In bed by 11pm.

MONDAY 1ST SEPTEMBER

Day off, so I may be able to go into Nicosia for the afternoon. That means instead of corned beef and mash I will feast at one of the restaurants – meat, mashed potatoes, peas, onions, the lot! Why can't we have that at camp instead of 'toad-in-the-hole' or egg and beans, sometimes fish and chips, but not very often.

I find a roller-skating rink and try it with the lads. We quite enjoy the skating, but there are Cypriots, Turks and Greeks there and we have to behave ourselves towards them, because it would be awkward if any of our service lads were involved in any trouble. We just go for the night out and stay calm and stay away from any conflict between the Greeks, Turks and Cypriots. Our service police are always on patrol, but Nicosia has been very quiet lately, anyway we have to be back at camp for 11pm.

We make our way to the transport back to our wadi and to bed. I must say it's a nice change to enjoy a good day out after slogging up to the aerodrome for days.

TUESDAY 2ND SEPTEMBER

The siren goes off at 4.30am. Itie aircraft are dropping flares and we rush to the trenches in pyjamas, boots and topcoats. It is pretty cold at this time in the morning. What a great way to be woken up! It's like daylight out here with all these blasted flares. Now they're dropping bombs, but they are falling miles away from us. It seems they have a job to find from us up there. We are definitely well camouflaged according to our pilots, and they should know, after all they fly over here all the time and know every spot of Cyprus. Incidentally, all the historical places are out of bounds to us, unfortunately. Just typical isn't it? We travel all this way from England and we can't even have a peep. Perhaps some day I might return as a tourist, who knows...

I wonder if our squadron will take part in the Western Desert campaign. We keep hearing on the radio that our troops have advanced, only to be pushed back, and that Auchinleck has had his ups and downs, especially in the Delta area.

There go the guns around Famagusta harbour where our fleet is moored. It seems either the Germans or the Ities have dropped a stick or two of bombs, but the harbour is well camouflaged with nets and there are dummy ships and wooden tanks, lorries, etc. I think I'll retire, there goes the all-clear.

WEDNESDAY 3RD SEPTEMBER

After last night's panic it seems that very little damage was done in Famagusta, which is just as well, it is our main port and all military supplies for the Navy, Army and Airforce, including our food, arrives there.

Some day I can see the Greek Cypriots and Turkish Cypriots having a go at each other, perhaps earlier than we think. We have to be on guard, and not talk of politics to any Cypriot. There are rumours that Cypriots have been asking troops for arms and military equipment of any kind, for which they will pay any price. We have had talks on this subject by our Squadron Leader and we were shocked to know what was going on. Let's get to that bleeding western desert, and the sooner the better! Even though we will be fighting Germans and Ities, at least we will know who we are up against.

THURSDAY 4TH SEPTEMBER

Up at 5.30 am, breakfast at 6am. We have to be at Nicosia aerodrome by 7am to re-arm and bomb-up. Our squadron is meeting up with bombers from African landing grounds to bomb some shipping in the Med. According to what our pilots tell us there's quite a convoy belonging to Jerry travelling and making for somewhere to invade some parts of the African coast. That's all they would say, I must admit we were getting a little bored these last few days. This certainly has giving us all a boost. Let's hope all of our lads will return…

They are airborne now, eight of them and just going out of sight, all aircraft are fitted with long range tanks. So back to our armoury stripping and cleaning guns for next operation should there be an emergency.

We have heard when we go up into the desert it's possible we may be re-equipped with 20mm cannons on the Hurricanes. What will they think of next.

I wonder if some day this aerodrome of Nicosia will be an important airport. At the moment there's just our armourer's hut made out of wood, something like a big shed, surrounded by empty petrol drums filled with sand from Kyrenia beach for protection against shrapnel. There are a few sand bunkers protecting our aircraft, otherwise just a hard sandy runway and hard rock under the sand, a few palm trees and a shooting range to test the guns. We keep the guns serviced very well; after all, a pilot's life depends on his guns operating without any trouble should he encounter the enemy.

I can hear sound of aircraft, they are 'ours' alright because they have fired the 'colours of the day' so that our anti-aircraft boys don't open fire at our own aircraft. Our pilots were delighted with their operation over the Med, unfortunately it must be kept secret. No long range tanks jettisoned, all bomb and ammo gone. Cameras are removed and film taken to be developed.

The squadron pilots have a scoreboard since arriving on Cyprus: 6 aircraft shot down, 5 trains strafed, 20 lorries bombed. That does not include today's sortie. Perhaps tomorrow we will know what damage they've done. Not a bad tally for just half a squadron; I think we do very well.

Back to work, re-arming, cleaning barrels of guns and casings of Brownings, checking for defects anywhere until everything is OK and ready for the next sortie. After 22 hours work we are ready for transport back to camp at 10.30pm, in bed by 11pm after a good supper.

FRIDAY 5TH SEPTEMBER

Day off. I may have a run into Nicosia to brighten up my spirits, I must admit we all get homesick, which is only natural, with the mail taking so long to arrive out here – sometimes three months – then we have a pile to answer. I decide to forget about mail for the moment and enjoy myself in Nicosia. It's amazing seeing Greeks, Turks and Cypriots sitting engrossed with ancient games that have been played here for many centuries. They sit for hours and drink their special coffee with wine added. Of course, there are the hubbly-bubbly pipes - a big glass bottle with a tube leading into a bottle, something like the shape of a vase with container on top for tobacco. Not for me, I'll find a place to eat and settle down to eggs, chips and bacon... very enjoyable! I visit some places where Saint Paul made a pilgrimage. Strange to imagine you are walking in his footsteps. King Richard The Lionheart also walked in many parts of Nicosia. Time seems to be pass quickly with so many interesting places, full of history. It's terrible to see all the orchards and vineyards for miles and miles full of fruit lying on the ground, going rotten. There are no ships available to take them all over the world like they used to, they have all been pressed into service for moving troops and equipment.

I arrived back in camp and stayed up to write this. Time now 1.45am. Oh, I nearly forgot - Richard The Lionheart married here, a lady by the name of Berengaria of Navarre, after which she was crowned Queen of England.

SATURDAY 6TH SEPTEMBER

It seems that I've caught some virus, I am too weak to move out of my camp bed according to our RAF doctor. Sweat just pours out of me, so I have to stay in bed for a couple of days and rest. At first he thought I had malaria, but he's diagnosed a touch of flu, so for the next couple of days some of the lads are bringing me my meals. What do you know, there goes the siren and I can hardly move so if the tent goes up, I'll be on my way to heaven! By the sound of it he is dropping plenty. Oh, to be home. At times like this, I miss my good mother and my lovely warm bed. Right now, though through the flap of the tent, there's a beautiful sunset. If only I could fly away, right now, in my mind, among those white clouds. Being ill in a place like this really gets you down. You think of what you left behind and wonder whether you will ever see home again and what might happen to you in this bloody war. I find that having a bit of a cry helps relieve the homesickness. Thank God, the siren's gone for all-clear. I'm writing this in my camp bed, it's like being on a camel to do it. Night's drawing near, so I'll put my home-made paraffin lamp on. At the moment I'm bloody fed up. Why can't these politicians fight their wars between themselves? I'm still awake at 2.30am. No work for another day, all I can do is sweat.

SUNDAY 7TH SEPTEMBER

Just finished my breakfast; porridge, bacon and egg, with the help of lads in tent. The tent accommodates three persons, which is just as well. I reckon if I had been in bivouac on my own I'd probably starve, as no one would bring me any food. It is 8.30am. I will be glad when I feel a little better and can move about. The doctor came at 10.30, he says to stay in bed, but if I pick up he wants to check me over at his surgery, which is a big tent, then I can be active and some use to the squadron, instead of being on my back.

5.50pm I've been to see the doctor and he says I'm serviceable and ready for any action. I can go for my own meals now, so I've sacked my 'butlers'!

There seems to be a panic at the aerodrome. All ground staff from tomorrow will be occupied for some time to come. We even have to sleep there, only transported back to camp for meals. I'll finish now, it's 12.30pm.

MONDAY 8TH SEPTEMBER

All ground staff up by 5.30am, breakfast 6.30am, then off the aerodrome. All our military forces are on alert all around the island. We are expecting an invasion from sea and air, so now we are on 24-hour stand-by in case Germans or Ities drop paratroops. So that means we sleep here in the armoury, fully clothed with our bayonets and rifles ready for use if need be. It's my life or the enemy's, so should it happen I'll use my bayonet if necessary to defend myself. I can hear the big guns firing at what looks like enemy aircraft above us. They haven't dropped any bombs, so they must be on reconnaissance. We are well fortified and the Ities will be in for a shock if they do mount an invasion, especially with part of our fleet and an aircraft carrier just off Cyprus. 1.45am, siren for all clear.

TUESDAY 9TH SEPTEMBER

At 8am, down to camp for our breakfast. I feel whacked, but we are fighting men and we just have to keep going. If the Germans take Cyprus they will have the Mediterranean under their control. Our own aircraft will not attempt to take off until the vital command is given. It seems to be a cat and mouse game; we are waiting for a golden opportunity to give them hell.

WEDNESDAY 10TH SEPTEMBER

We slept on the aerodrome all night. We heard one or two enemy aircraft above at different times. We still have our clothes on after 24 hours on stand-by. I sometimes wonder if our squadron may be a decoy, because we only have small part to play in the Mediterranean. Food now is being made at the aerodrome rather than waste time bringing it by transport. Our pilots are ready should any notice be given. All ground crew have to make certain the guns on the aircraft and cameras are all in working order. So now it's up to the pilots' ability. How I wish to be with them, I can imagine sitting in the cockpit, they certainly have guts, especially thinking - 'will it be possible to return?' There goes the siren for them to take off, already eight pilots have been in their cockpits for an hour. Away they go, like a flock of seagulls. The object for them is to strafe and bomb Rhodes, Karpathos and Kasos, a tough job all round, especially with German and Itie aircraft of all kinds about. However, they are too busy flying from Crete having a crack at Libyan aerodromes for the moment. Oh yes, I should have mentioned, about our first sorties. Our squadron isn't organised as such, like having individual pilots. That's why I've never mentioned any pilot's name because at the moment anyone takes any aircraft. Perhaps when we get a chance in the western desert, but for now when our squadron leader picks anyone for sorties it could be anybody, although I find working like this provides comradeship successfully and very well at that. The officers here are great, all like the lads - no bull!

THURSDAY 11TH SEPTEMBER

At least as an armourer I stand more chance of seeing the future than the pilots; their life expectancy is not good at all. Still, all our aircraft returned yesterday with just minor repairs needed on one or two. Today we have stand-down. We still have some pilots with us who flew out from the aircraft carrier *Furious*.

FRIDAY 12TH SEPTEMBER

It's a great pity that pilots are not assigned to individual aircraft, so the ground crews can get to know them by name, but that's impossible, they may be posted to another squadron at short notice because of the loss of pilots in the Western Desert. We don't know what's going to happen, we could be moving at any time...

SATURDAY 13TH SEPTEMBER

I am listening to a load of bull from Churchill. "We will fight in the streets and the hills, no matter where the fighting is." It makes you laugh because it's not Churchill who will win the war; our saviours will be the officers and men who do the dirty work. According to him, after the war we will all have a decent standard of living. I wonder whether that will come true...

Our squadron has had a day's stand-down; there is very little activity today, just lounging about and resting and no 'surprises' from any Itie or German aircraft.

SUNDAY 14TH SEPTEMBER

We keep waiting for word for our squadron to move to the Western Desert, but it never comes. Sometimes I wonder if we are just a decoy. At the moment we are just killing time, stripping guns, keeping them in order, and maintaining bomb racks and flare pistols for colours of the day. Better than letting them rust. So for now it's a relaxing time we are having.

MONDAY 15TH SEPTEMBER

Same as yesterday. Doing a spot of washing to occupy myself. We have had one or two alarms, aircraft above, but only Ities. It's when Jerry comes that there's a panic – their long-range Messerschmitt 100 twin engined bombers are far superior to any Itie aircraft – then we have flares, bombs, the lot...

There's no doubting the Germans' engineering skills, or the skill of their pilots. What the hell are we doing killing each other – for what? Bloody nothing!

TUESDAY 16TH SEPTEMBER

Panic. Start work at 5am, reloading .303 ammunition into eight Hurricanes, ready for emergency stand-by. They took off at 11 o'clock. Enemy aircraft are approaching the island and at the moment we are on the alert because you never know how far away these aircraft are. Our planes have been away a couple of hours, let's hope things work out all right.

It looks like our aircraft are back. My pilot says that they shot down four Italian aeroplanes. I take the camera out of the leading edge to take to the photographic tent, but we definitely won't see the pictures; only the pilot will. I take off the panel to get at the guns, clean and reload and they're ready for action again, perhaps tomorrow if there's another panic. All our aircraft have returned safely and our pilots congratulate the ground crew for keeping things in good condition. Well done 213 Squadron

WEDNESDAY 17TH SEPTEMBER

Time does certainly drag, especially when you start thinking about what you could be doing at home, enjoying yourself instead of sitting under a palm tree!

I must admit, the scenery here is absolutely beautiful and it's quite warm. We are on stand-down, so I take this opportunity to relax; why waste such a lovely panoramic view? I may possibly have a nap – if our sirens don't start up – before returning to the aerodrome, which is only a five-minute walk from here, then wait till transport comes to take us back to camp, which is a bit safer from enemy aircraft. Camp is situated in what they call a 'wadi' – a dried up river bed.

THURSDAY 18TH SEPTEMBER

We are spending the day in Kyrenia, which has a fantastic bay for swimming in a lovely sandy beach; it's a picnic outing and a chance to relax away from the aerodrome and planes. The water is as clear as anything, and the sea and sky are a pure blue. Today is very clear and we can see the coast of Turkey. I'm having a cup of tea, some eats, which were provided by our super cook, and I'm quite enjoying myself.

On our way back we call in for a cup of tea and some good old English cooking at the garden cafe owned by the two old ladies. They make you very at home. God bless them! We return back to camp after a very enjoyable day, now off to bed, 11pm.

FRIDAY 19TH SEPTEMBER

I have just come back from Nicosia and everything's quiet, but there are rumours about increased friction between Turks and Greeks. They are still trying to get hold of arms and military supplies via the black market. Our officers say the arms would not to be used against us, they are for when this war is over, then the Greeks and Turks will start off their own little war. I do believe it could happen, I must say they do seem to mean business, but it's strange because they seem like such nice people. Religion and politics are the cause of so much fighting, and that won't ever change.

SATURDAY 20TH SEPTEMBER

Back at the aerodrome. The Sappers and Durham Light Infantry are still trying to shape the runway; they are doing a great job.

SUNDAY 21ST SEPTEMBER

Another day of rest and peace. Our life here changes so much from day to day, you never know what's going to happen. If I survive this bloody useless war, I promise I will bring Doris to this beautiful jewel of the Med. If only God will only fulfil my prayer and spare me.*

MONDAY 22ND SEPTEMBER

The news of the war's progress never seems to be very good. I try not to think too much about it, because it makes me miserable, so I try to think of all the things I will be able to do after peace returns.

Summer is over and nights are very cold. Squadron Leader McDonald gave us a pep talk today, saying that the squadron ground crews have worked exceedingly well and he's pleased with us. Perhaps it won't be long before we leave Cyprus to see action in the Western Desert. We will all be working day and night, looking forward to that occasion.

TUESDAY 23RD SEPTEMBER

There is still a lot of friction between the Greeks and Turks. Some shepherds came to the edge of the aerodrome and we had a chat with them (they speak a little English). They told us they are pleased the English are here, otherwise the Turks would try and take over. They say that when we go away, a war will start. I tried convincing them that it will not happen, but they kept saying "bloody Turks, robbers of our country!"

---

*In April 1986 Doris and I finally did holiday in Cyprus together. We visited Nicosia, but I couldnt find anything to remind me of my wartime years there.

The Greeks seem very sociable people, but we seldom seem to come in contact with the Turks, they are more to the north.

Our squadron has had an easy day, sort of relaxed, but winter weather's just around the corner.

WEDNESDAY 24TH SEPTEMBER

The siren's going like mad, it looks like German or Itie reconnaissance aircraft. They are too high to identify, but I've never seen so many over the island. There's word of some shipping coming into Famagusta with quite a lot of supplies for our forces, so perhaps they are after that. No bombs dropped; two hours in our trenches, then all clear sounds.

THURSDAY 25TH SEPTEMBER

We are heading for the winter months and it's starting to get cold, something like the winter back home in England. I am looking out from our armoury across the aerodrome and trying to imagine what it was like here when Alexander the Great was here. There are traces left here by Phoenicians, Greeks, Romans, Crusaders, Lusignans, Venetians and many others. Cyprus is an island whose turbulent history is as dramatic and compelling as anywhere in the world; an island where the mythical gods and goddesses of ancient Greece indulged themselves in pleasure and tragedy; where Aphrodite, goddess of love and beauty, emerged from the foam; whence came the word *Philoxenia*, meaning 'friendship towards strangers';

where Jesus' disciples came to preach the Lord's word. What a wonderful place! I enjoy a lovely evening of imagination and beauty before retiring to bed, a perfect night, and no aircraft about 12.30am.

FRIDAY 26TH SEPTEMBER

The siren is going again – a squadron of Heinkel IIIs is approaching Cyprus, too late for our squadron to take off, but fortunately our aircraft are well dispersed and camouflaged. There are plenty of ack-ack guns around the island so they won't attempt any low flying. We can see them, very high up, six Heinkels. I think they are after the shipping. They drop their bombs out at sea and just do a reconnaissance flight over us, hoping to see something, and are soon gone. Thank the Lord, there goes the all clear! We seem to be getting these spasms of enemy activity lately. Our pilots are taking it easy for the moment, and why not, they work hard enough when they are airborne. I'm writing a few letters home, it's almost 12.45am. Then I'll retire to dreamland.

SATURDAY 27TH SEPTEMBER

We are on stand-down for three days, preparing all our aircraft to be in tip-top condition, ready for action at short notice if necessary. We keep thinking of threats from the islands Germany occupies, around the Mediterranean, one never knows what might happen. We are prepared for anything in combat. The days seem long and boredom sets in now and again. Down at our camp, away from the aerodrome we have a canteen where we can have a few drinks and listen to the radio, but it's always the same surroundings. We play cards, etc, then it's time for bed. This bloody war seems to change everybody quite a bit, however right now I'm feeling sleepy, so good night, God bless.

SUNDAY 28TH SEPTEMBER

Some of our squadron has been sent to help Nos 80 and 260 Squadrons in Lydda, Palestine, strafing and bombing Meskine, Takia and Aleppo airfields, with success, apparently. We are left with only eight aircraft. One of our planes flew off *HMS Furious*, the aircraft carrier, and lost its way to Abu Sueir, Egypt. It arrived safely to be attached to 73 Squadron and did well, shooting down four ME109s, also damaged ME110. It flew with 73 Squadron, strafing enemy tanks and transport in the Bardia area in Egypt, still there, I didn't get pilot's name. Perhaps some day the whole squadron will be together again.

MONDAY 29TH SEPTEMBER

What a night! I came back from Nicosia, got into bed, and straight away the air-raid siren went. I jumped for my life. The full moon gave the enemy aircraft a grand view below, and they started dropping flares and bombs. I was in our trench by then. The bombs seemed to be coming down near Famagusta and Kyrenia. The raid went on for two hours, then the planes disappeared. Despite the full moon, they missed our aerodrome; it was too well camouflaged, with all the aircraft safely hidden under nets.

Got up, had breakfast, then was transported up to the aerodrome. All hell was let loose from 12pm until 6pm. Itie aircraft never stopped bombing but still didn't hit any of our aircraft, or any part of the drome. They were too high, but if they had come any lower our guns would have blasted them out of the sky. When things calmed down a bit, our aircraft took off and chased them, shooting down two of their bombers. All of our aircraft returned safely. Things returned back to normal! Amen!

TUESDAY 30TH SEPTEMBER

Up early at 5.30am for breakfast, then away to the aerodrome. There's a panic on. Four of our aircraft are ready to take off to engage four incoming Itie bombers. There they go, into the Mediterranean sky, what a performance as our pilots manoeuvre into position and head out to sea. We see one of the Itie bombers diving to avoid our fighters, but his aircraft's already on fire, one of our pilots must have hit him. We don't see anybody bale out. The other three enemy aircraft managed to disappear into cloud and scarpered. All our Hurricanes returned safely. All guns worked well, so there was praise for the ground crews from the pilots. I wrote some letters home, and that's me for the night.

WEDNESDAY 1ST OCTOBER

Religion and politics continue to make for a very sensitive situation between the Greeks and Turks. We have had a pep talk from our Squadron Leader, telling us to be very careful about which areas we visit when in Nicosia, and to keep out of the Turkish areas and keep to the Greek ones. We British have had no trouble so far. They certainly keep good cafes and cater well for the troops. We have had a rest period from the aerodrome today, and I'm writing this after coming back from town. I'm making my bed, just blankets and no sheets, but never mind, I still sleep well.

THURSDAY 2ND OCTOBER

Its so cold you would think this was England, believe me it's hard to believe we are in the middle of the Mediterranean. We are on stand-to from 5.30am at the aerodrome. By 6.30am our planes are taking off to intercept enemy aircraft approaching Cyprus, the pilots won't tell us their objective, but it seems something is up. All troops are on alert. We see some Focke-Wulf 200s, equipped with FUG Hohentwiel search radar, quite a big aircraft, Junkers 87s, and Heinkel 111 KG4s, but too high for any identification. There is quite a bit of ack-ack going full blast. Our aircraft have engaged the enemy with other squadron based at Larnaca, which has just been made into a landing strip. The Germans weren't expecting an easy approach and all scarpered this time. Their airforce seems to be getting bigger all the time. They must be operating from somewhere along the coast of North Africa. Here comes our squadron, back home at last, no damage thank

God, not even a shot; the Germans were well prepared for a getaway run. Who knows what they may do next time, we know their air force is building up in a big way all over the Mediterranean. But for now I'll relax and sleep well tonight.

FRIDAY 3RD OCTOBER

One thing about this war, you never know what's coming next, especially when it comes to German aircraft. Lately, we have been seeing a different type of reconnaissance plane, quite big, so they are probably long range aircraft coming from quite a distance. They seem to be different every time they come. Six of our aircraft took off to investigate what they were up to, but one of our stand-by pilots says that our aircraft are not capable of achieving the altitudes reached by the German planes, which are Dornier 17E, Dornier 17E 111 and Dornier 17P-1s, apparently. Our aircraft have returned and the German planes have disappeared. What the hell are they up to?

SATURDAY 4TH OCTOBER

I've only just got out of bed, 7.30am and the bloody sirens are going full blast, so we have to dive into our trenches, not even time to go to the toilet. Yesterday we had Germans, today we have Italian bombers dropping their loads. They were Savoia Marchetti SM 79/EX1s, four of them, classed as long-range bombers. Thank God our pilots chased them off but no victories for our lads, although one of the enemy aircraft was hit by the ack-ack when flying low. One stick of bombs hit the aerodrome but did not cause much damage, just two holes on edge of the airstrip and an old cottage other side of Nicosia. It seems that their intention is to strike and run like hell. I must say their bomb-aiming skills are hopeless, but this is good news for us. According to our pilots, their instruments are poor quality, but they may have new equipment and techniques in a few months time. We spent four hours in our trenches. Raid like this do shake you a bit. Roll on Blighty! Went to Nicosia, back by 10, made tea, then to bed.

SUNDAY 5TH OCTOBER

Stand-to done for 14 days to get all our aircraft operational. Our first duty was to get everything out of the gun bays, also cameras, and look for any cracks on mounts or metal structures. We must be very observant because after 14 days we may be on the move. I'll believe it when I see it, we've had so many disappointments. Spent all day on inspection of three aircraft; we all knocked off at 8pm, storms and sand blowing, never stopping. All aircraft had to be covered, now here's the rain, what next? Summer's gone so wrap up Jack, we have switched back to wearing our RAF blue uniforms. No sirens today, early in bed. Our Flight Sergeant's a great fellow, he's talking about having a night out with the lads – that would never happen in England – anyway, I'll look forward to it.

MONDAY 6TH OCTOBER

Another hectic day. Arrived at aerodrome 8.30am. Worked on dismantling guns, taking them out of the bays, inspecting for defects. Looking around the bench all I can see are Browning guns and cases. The weather's terrible outside the armoury, which is only made of wood and tin, though compared to what some of the Cypriots live in, our accommodation is the Hilton Hotel! Two of us sleep inside for security, either the Cypriots or the Turks would just love all these guns and ammunition. There are also guns for aircraft, rifles, flares and hand grenades. What a ball they would have with that little lot! Of course, our aerodrome is well guarded by the RAF Regiment, but we do have a loaded rifle at the ready when on duty and have orders to use it if necessary should anyone attempt breaking in. Fortunately, I've never had the opportunity to use the weapon, I'm not the killer type, although maybe, if forced, I might consider pulling the trigger. We work shifts, the next two armourers take over and do inspections, as we have done, ready to put the guns back into the aircraft. What we have on the bench will take four or five days yet. My mate and I have decided to call it a day, 12.30pm, bedtime.

TUESDAY 7TH OCTOBER

No peace for the wicked, the bloody siren has gone off at 4.30am. They mean business. We jump into covered trenches and have to stay put for over 3 hours. They are dive-bombing and strafing, it's like Blackpool Illuminations, but we are well camouflaged and hard to see, even with flares. Our pilots say that even by daylight, if we didn't signal with our day flares, they would find it hard to see us. Nearly 8am, all clear has sounded and no damage done, no-idea what type of enemy aircraft. The worst part of it was that it's pissing down and I'm wet through (no, I haven't, thank you!). We are waiting for our stand-down. It's hard to find words to describe our activities on a day-to-day basis, especially when we never move from same spot. It's still raining cats and dogs, I'm writing this in a tent shared by six. I've rested during the afternoon. Time now 10.30pm. Bloody cold, I'm away to get to a warm bed.

WEDNESDAY 8TH OCTOBER

Six of our aircraft took off to engage enemy bombers before they could approach the island, this seems to be very odd because they usually wait until they're near the coast, however we can see them and they look like reconnaissance planes, because they're too high for dropping bombs. There's no doubt they are trying something out - can't see any more now. Sirens go - all clear. Our aircraft all return and when the pilots get out of their cockpits, what a tale they tell. They were definitely German aircraft, and our lot followed them out to sea but could not catch them because they shot like bolts out of hell, it seems. On each wing were to rocket-shaped pieces of equipment. Our pilots have never seen anything like them, impossible to bring them to combat. Thank the Lord none of our pilots was lost. Another hectic day over and it's bloody cold! We are using our mosquito nets, what with them and the Jerries, it's hard to tell who has got the worst sting! Good night all, it's bed time again - socks on!

THURSDAY 9TH OCTOBER

The rain here is worse than in England, outside it's a quagmire. It has rained for 82 hours, but it gives me time to write home. I hope the sirens don't go today, our dugouts are well covered with a frame on top and sandbags just at the side of wadi. You would think there was a waterfall gushing down towards Nicosia. No signs of enemy aircraft, so it's a stay-in day, and miserable. I light my home-made lamp, paraffin and string, to see what I'm writing about. Bed's the only warm place on nights like this - socks on again!

FRIDAY 10TH OCTOBER

I'm sick of lying on these cane beds, I've decided to make my own frame bed out of timber from engine crates. Some of the officers want me to make beds for them, too, with two or three old sacks stretched over frames for a mattress – a bit softer than cane. I made 10 and all went to satisfied customers. I also made a few tables for lamps, etc, so I made a nice little profit.

SATURDAY 11TH OCTOBER

These sandstorms don't improve things any and the weather's shocking. We have a job to keep warm in our tents. Warrant Officer in charge of armoury, Lewis, gave us a little talk at 2pm, about precautions and safety, a secret talk and it was out of the blue. He told us to watch out for booby traps dropped by enemy aircraft during the raids: cameras, pens, watches, rubbers, brooches, any item we might see lying down, to leave it alone. He also congratulated us on the performance of each armourer in keeping guns on the aircraft in perfect order throughout our stay in Cyprus. Especially when we have sandstorms. He also spoke of comradeship which they seem to lack back home, reason, too much bullshit! Definitely right. Out here we get on with the job and we're not bothered with little Hitlers making us polish buttons and shoes or put our caps on straight. Thank God we're away from that! Of course, we don't neglect ourselves or our squadron, that's why our pilots appreciate what we are doing, keeping them alive and not wasting our time on bull.

SUNDAY 12TH OCTOBER

What a panic, everybody's out on the camp and aerodrome, sirens-full blast, we can hear quite a few enemy aeroplanes. We are all ready with rifles and bayonets, preparing for an invasion. From a distance it looks as though enemy parachutists have been dropped. We are in our trenches ready for an attack. All hell is let loose by the heavy flak on the island. The RAF Regiment and Army are on full alert. Two hours have gone by, seemingly the enemy has only dropped booby traps, dummies and decoys. A few have been destroyed at Famagusta, Trudos, Larnaca, Ayia Napa, Karavostassi.

Sirens go, all clear. They dropped 14 dummies, six of our aircraft took off for the raid but bombers were too high to catch. Our planes returned safely, no guns fired. They were up against Dornier reconnaissance planes again.

MONDAY 13TH OCTOBER

Today is very quiet. I think Jerry took too much on yesterday and it surprised him with all the flak, I won't be jumping into trenches today and getting wet, a good night's sleep for once.

TUESDAY 14TH OCTOBER

Rumours are circulating around about change of planes from Mk I Hawker Hurricanes with eight guns to Mk IIc Hurricanes with 20mm cannons in preparation for desert warfare. We will have to wait and see. I work at the aerodrome cleaning guns on two aircraft and the day has been very quiet for a change. It's much nicer this way, even our pilots are having a rest day. My mate and I are on duty, so we'll be sleeping in the tin hut. It's now 10 in the evening, finished maintenance on aircraft. Doing a bit of reading then off to sleep.

WEDNESDAY 15TH OCTOBER

From now on we are on stand-by at aerodrome, in case German and Ities start building up their aircraft, especially on the islands they occupy. However, no raids today, thank God.

THURSDAY 16TH OCTOBER

Stand by, air raid siren goes. Nothing happens. Stand by our aircraft all day but no action. Sirens went and enemy aircraft sighted, but went off peacefully.

FRIDAY 17TH OCTOBER

Still on aerodrome cleaning barrels and making sure all guns are serviceable for action.

SATURDAY 18TH OCTOBER

WAR DECLARED ON AMERICA! We have to carry our rifles at all times from today and also bayonets. Believe me it causes tense feelings, especially at night. There are RAF Regiment and Army patrols through the night, we have to know the password, and should anyone forget, they could be shot! What next? Now and again we have the army in our armoury for a cup of tea.

SUNDAY 19TH OCTOBER

These Cypriots are in a panic over possibility of an invasion, they keep asking if we think there will be one. We just say that we don't think so. Word has come through to the operations radio van to look out for German fighter aircraft. They are a lot faster and have greater manoeuvrability than our British fighters, so our pilots will need to use 100 per cent of their skills if they want to stay alive. The Messerschmitt BF 109-2 is the cream of the

German air force. We might see them, should we get the opportunity, in the western desert. We'll sleep on it.

MONDAY 20TH OCTOBER

There goes that bleeding siren! I see enemy aircraft well above but hardly able to identify. Our squadron scrambled to pursue aircraft above. No bombs dropped or any other action, it seems they are after the shipping at Famagusta. We can hear the ack-ack, and see flares in the sky. Our squadron returns from operations but the pilots say the German long range bombers were flying too high and our fighters couldn't get near them to do battle. Once more, quite an easy day for ground staff. Reports come through that the ack-ack guns shot enemy aircraft down on bomb run. Seemingly there were two waves of bombers. No

The author (front row, squatting) plus other 213 Squadron armourers, Nicosia, Cyprus, 1941.

damage to our aerodrome - lucky us! Time now 11.15pm, time for bed.

TUESDAY 21ST OCTOBER

I wonder when all this will end as the days go on (time might tell). I have a day off so we are off to Kyrenia for a good old swim, it's really not bad weather at the moment. Called on those old English ladies. What good cooking! Apple pie, blackberry pie and selection of trifles and custards – just like home! It was a very pleasant afternoon under the lovely trees of oranges, lemons, and figs, it was fantastic. What a good day. I will sleep well tonight.

WEDNESDAY 22ND OCTOBER

Stand down for 24 hours, unless there are emergencies. Taking it easy.

THURSDAY 23RD OCTOBER

Stand by for any emergency at aerodrome, it seems the Middle East war offensive is building up and both side's reinforcements are being targeted. Everything seems to be building up for a big push.

FRIDAY 24TH OCTOBER

The siren's blasting at 3am. The whole night sky is lit up with flares. I rush to put trousers and overcoat on over my pyjamas, and with unlaced boots, one big leap into the trench. Bombs are dropping but they seem quite a way off, it looks as if Famagusta's getting the worst of it again. The German planes are Dornier 17 P-1 (F22), a reconnaissance and long range bomber. It's now 6am, there goes the all clear. The rest of the day no action, a bit of peace and in bed by 10pm.

SATURDAY 25TH OCTOBER

It's absolutely belting down, a very miserable day. Outside the tents are pools of water, as if we didn't have enough to put up with in this bloody war, never knowing what is to happen next. Roll on that bloody boat for home – amen!

SUNDAY 27TH OCTOBER

There go those blasted sirens at an unearthly hour, 4.30am. We rush out to trenches in haste. You would think there was a full moon, with the light from all the flares dropping. We hear the drone of engines in the sky. Fortunately no bombs dropped. I can't understand why they send so many reconnaissance planes, surely they must know by now what air force we have here. All clear goes at 7.30am, in time for breakfast.

MONDAY 28TH OCTOBER

It's really cold and miserable, however, we are on a night duty in our tin hut armoury, with a lovely big fire, doing a spot of writing home. Let's hope no Jerries drop in for supper! Anyway, we are ready with rifles and bayonets, so we would give them a right reception! Cypriots are a little afraid when we are in cafes, they come over and ask if the Germans will come here. We say 'no, never' trying to persuade them all is well. It's 3.30am, writing by Tilley lamp - no electric. That's all for now, I'm away to bed.

TUESDAY 29TH OCTOBER

Away to breakfast, 7.30am, and quite a lovely morning. Looking towards the horizon how beautiful it looks, how panoramic, out of this world, especially at this time of morning. So peaceful. Why can't human beings be like that, instead of all this violence, fear and hate for one another? Love is a forgotten word in these times, especially the Turks and Greeks. Fortunately, I don't think they like the idea of a German occupation and and so they are behaving themselves. Both Greeks and Turks tell us that they would prefer the English to occupy their country. It's hard to believe there's a war on today, it's so peaceful, probably not for long. Very little action today, only killing scorpions and flies.

WEDNESDAY 30TH OCTOBER

Stand down today. I'll have a bath in one of the empty ammunition tins, it holds about one gallon of water, we are rationed to three gallons a week and that means my dirty laundry will be washed in my bathwater. Fortunately we go for a swim at Kyrenia once a week should it be fine, and if not, we make the best of what we've got. We have a shower made from a petrol can using rainwater from a drum, and it works very well, so I'm not so dirty, but oh for a good old hot bath. My ironing board is my bed, and I'm the iron, with the heat coming from my body! A very quiet day which is unusual.

THURSDAY 31ST OCTOBER

There go the sirens and off go six of our Hurricanes. We can hear the enemy aircraft above, they are just specks in the sky, can't see what type. Three have dispersed in different directions to attract our fighters away from the ones behind. Our fighters return back to aerodrome, no bombs dropped or any losses. Our planes never used their guns - our pilots still say that the German aircraft are superior to any in the world, although that's their opinion, so we leave it at that.

FRIDAY 1ST NOVEMBER

Squadron Leader Lockhart is trying to get the whole squadron back together. Our planes have destroyed 20 enemy aircraft so far, both here in Cyprus and in North Africa, at Sidi Hanaish when part of 213 Squadron is attached to 73 Squadron.

SATURDAY 2ND NOVEMBER

We may be all together shortly as rumours are circulating that we're making for Egypt and the western desert. Some of our Sergeant Pilots look to be no more than 18 or 20. What a waste of youth. Why should these lads, or anyone else, have to be sacrificed for the sake of the stupid people who are in power.

SUNDAY 3RD NOVEMBER

I must admit we haven't had as much action here in Cyprus as the other half of our squadron out in the western desert. From what we hear on the radio they are kept very, very active. Its 10.30pm and it's like daylight out there, with enemy aircraft dropping flares and bombs. It sounds like there's quite a few planes but it always seems to be Famagusta that gets the worst of it. Ships keep coming and going, and we hear they are preparing for a big push. Our pilots have been keeping very quiet, especially at night, with no take offs from aerodrome, that might give our position away.

MONDAY 4TH NOVEMBER

Part of B Flight has moved to Port Said, patrolling over shipping in the Mediterranean which just leaves a few of us here in Cyprus. This could mean that we could all form together again on the mainland ready for the big push towards the western desert. We have been told that our squadron will be participating in this theatre of war within the next few weeks. There go the sirens and all hell's let loose from our Bofors and anti- aircraft guns. The RAF Regiment are on the alert with the Army around our aerodrome. No bombs dropped on this raid.

TUESDAY 5TH NOVEMBER

Bonfire night, but we don't need to buy any fireworks, we see plenty from the Jerries and the Ities when they come, every colour of pyrotechnics imaginable in the skies. Fortunately, our enemy pals are having a night off, no raids. I went into Nicosia this afternoon; at one of the cafes a Greek approached us asking for guns and grenades, but he saw one of their policemen and ran away. Arrived back at camp at 11pm, dog-tired.

WEDNESDAY 6TH NOVEMBER

Our German friends paid us another hostile visit. We had to dive into our trenches after they dropped quite a few screamer bombs, but they still missed our aerodrome. The flak and Bofors guns are going like blazes all round Cyprus. Six of our aircraft intercepted and damaged two enemy planes, who then made out to sea, our pilots said that they possibly baled out, but seeing no aircraft in the sea, they probably sank. There goes the all clear after four hours of agony. Believe me, those screamers really test your nerves, it's really weird, it's our first attack like this. From now on we have been told, we might have to do night watch, which means sleeping under the aircraft, 24 hours on, 24 off.

THURSDAY 7TH NOVEMBER

I nearly forgot to mention, one of our sergeants recently made up to FO (Flying Officer). Since the squadron's been on this island he's had seven prangs. Ground crew have nick-named him Hopper Wallace, so if by chance we move to Egypt and the western desert and he gets shot down, with the practice he's had he won't need a parachute - pancakes are his speciality! Even the pilots have a name for him - Water Wings! Apart from that, they all have to learn from their mistakes. If I'm on duty I hope I'm awake when an approach is made by FO Wallace! We are hoping that all of our aircraft will be fitted with tropical filters beneath the noses when we move to Egypt.

FRIDAY 8TH NOVEMBER

Six of our long range Hurricanes are off to escort a convoy of ships in the Mediterranean, sailing into Alexandria, which could be loaded full of aeroplanes, tanks, lorries, ammunition, guns and other equipment. They have been away three hours. We hear aircraft, all six return safe, flying low over the aerodrome. Aircraft now taxiing into sand bays, none of the guns have been fired, pilots say it was a big convoy, but no sign of enemy aircraft, so all's well that ends well.

SATURDAY 9TH NOVEMBER

We hear on the radio that Blenheim aircraft are used in the desert war. There's one squadron of Boeing B17 Flying Fortresses operation from the Canal Zone, they are bombing Benghazi. Marylands also attacked Derna, these planes were attacked by fighters, identified as BF109s, and one was shot down, although we found out later another Maryland was lost. Only four Boeing B17s are being used in the desert theatre as an experiment. One was shot down and 238 Squadron was ordered to search for the plane and destroy it. After much searching the aircraft returned to base unsuccessful but in the event the crew of the Fortress made a reasonable job of destruction and walked back to the Allied lines. Our pilots told us that on no account must a Boeing B17 fall into German hands.

SUNDAY 10TH NOVEMBER

Operations in the Mediterranean are definitely coming to a head. General Wavell has strengthened his forces, to compete with Rommel's forces, who are preparing for a big push to Alexandria, but whatever the outcome we seem to be holding our own. We keep in contact with radio, more so now, because here in Cyprus we seem to be at a standstill. Wavell took over in July, 1939.

MONDAY 11TH NOVEMBER

It seems this war will be over before our squadron can take part. Some of our aircraft are in Syria, Palestine and Egypt.

TUESDAY 12TH NOVEMBER

There seems to be a lot of controversy on radio, about Japan maybe declaring war on America, also 253 Wing with Hurricanes and 208, 237, 451 Squadrons in the western desert, causing havoc on airfields, and also 33 and 272 Squadrons of Beaufighters destroyed quite a number of aircraft at Tmimi airfield including five JU52s taking off. All this action and we are stuck on Cyprus! 33 Squadron has Gladiators but they may transfer to Hurricanes at a later date.

WEDNESDAY 13TH NOVEMBER

It's what one would call a lazy day, sleeping, eating and just relaxing and writing one or two letters home. Off duty until Friday, fortunately we have had no raids, so it seems the Germans and Ities are concentrating on Cyrenaica and Libya.

THURSDAY 14TH NOVEMBER

Off to Kyrenia for the day and on return stopping off at Nicosia, and may have tea and supper in one of the cafes. Had a real good day, enjoyed every minute.

FRIDAY 15TH NOVEMBER

Early call, we have to be on alert. All ten of our aircraft are standing by for action. We have only 10 aeroplanes, the rest are scattered around the Mediterranean on loan to different squadrons. On the aerodrome by 5.30am, checking guns and bombs for a raid on Axis shipping making towards Derna or Tobruk. Perhaps they may try and land further down the coast. Off go all our aircraft. The convoy will probably be protected by German ME109-3s from Crete. Our aircraft return, all safe, taxi in, re-arm and bomb up, and away they go again. On the first raid all ammunition and bombs were used up. According to our pilots they've never seen as many aircraft in the sky. Two hours gone and we see our aircraft returning. Yes, they fire the colours of the day. All our pilots are home safe. They have done quite a bit of damage to the shipping, apparently. Enemy fighters did engage but were outnumbered, so now all our aircraft are grounded for inspections – they have done well.

SATURDAY 16TH NOVEMBER

All aircraft are having full inspections and two are having long range tanks fitted to go on a reconnaissance flight over Dodecanese Islands. It seems part of the Axis operation went that way and the other to North Africa. The two aircraft prepared for tomorrow have specially fitted cameras under the fuselage. We rearm guns again in case of emergency and check bomb racks. Almost finished at 10pm. We are sleeping on the aerodrome for the next few nights because there are rumours that Cyprus may be invaded. Highly improbable. Just in case we sleep with our clothes on.

SUNDAY 17TH NOVEMBER

Up at 7.30, have breakfast, and am ready for checks on guns and racks. Two reconnaissance aircraft took off early this morning. When they arrive back, according to the pilots, the Dodecanese Islands are swarming with military equipment of all kinds, so no doubt the Germans have something up their sleeves, but what, we will never be told. What a cold day, it's like an English winter. I sometimes sleep with my socks, trousers and pullover on when it's really bad.

MONDAY 18TH NOVEMBER

Up early to prepare for a long journey for two of our aircraft over Crete. Fitted with long range tanks they take off at 11.30am. Away three hours. Just hearing aircraft, yes, it's our two back from Crete. They taxi into their sandbag hangars. Photos perfect. It seems as though another island is well equipped with military equipment of all sorts. The Germans seem to be preparing for action in Middle East.

TUESDAY 19TH NOVEMBER

It's really cold, it must be, I'm wearing an overcoat and I'm still very cold. There is plenty of action with ack-ack guns all around the island. I think some of the enemy planes must have been decoys to see what defence there is around Cyprus. We stood in trenches for almost three hours before the all clear went.

WEDNESDAY 20TH NOVEMBER

Sometimes I wonder what we're doing out here, at least we don't have to worry about tanks coming after us, and long range guns, like in the Western desert. We are never on the run, we are almost static, but we do have German aircraft above us and also Italian.

THURSDAY 21ST NOVEMBER

Four of our flight are going on reconnaissance over the Aegean Sea, fitted with long range tanks. There are movements of German troops and there are airfields along that coast. We are on edge until we hear the sound of their return. They are back after four hours, all return safely without any opposition. Pilots say that it was a very successful flight.

FRIDAY 22ND NOVEMBER

The other half of 213 Squadron have been active all over the Middle East, Israel, Syria and Jordan. Apparently, there's friction in Palestine between the Arabs and the Jews, they just can't see eye to eye, let's hope we can try and control it, otherwise God only knows what will happen.

SATURDAY 23RD NOVEMBER

The prospect of going home to Blighty seems like a distant dream. Perhaps we'll die here.

SUNDAY 24TH NOVEMBER

There have been three Generals in command here: General Wavell, appointed 1939, then Cunningham, 1941, now we hear Ritchie is to take over. Part of our squadron is on patrol off Alexandria guarding our shipping coming into port from the Mediterranean. We seem to be a bit nearer to seeing some proper action – I wonder!

MONDAY 25TH NOVEMBER

Part of our squadron landed in Egypt last night, they were protecting a big convoy from England with more equipment for our advances towards the western desert. The ground crews from another squadron are maintaining 213 Squadron for their stay of three days. No raids here today, maybe German aircraft are diverting to the Mediterranean.

TUESDAY 26TH NOVEMBER

I must say we are more or less having a holiday, passing time away writing to friends at home; it makes me feel a little homesick, especially looking from inside my tent at the beautiful sunset resting on the horizon, and wondering what is going on in England. Why do we have to have bloody wars? We are still on stand-by with a few aircraft left. I've had a good dinner, tea and supper, now I'm off to bed, 1am.

WEDNESDAY 27TH NOVEMBER

Action stations. Early call to be on stand-by at the aerodrome by 6.30am. We must be expecting an attack on the ships approaching Famagusta. Four Hurricanes take off to engage three or four Savoia Marchetti SM 79/PXI, Italian torpedo bombers, from Greece. They are well equipped with an advanced technique for hitting their targets spot on. Our planes have been away two hours. They arrive back and the pilots tell us that they chased the bombers which dumped their bombs into the sea without any success. Our pilots did not use their guns, but we still have to inspect and clean them. Stand-down, left aerodrome at 11pm. Back to camp for supper, then to bed.

THURSDAY 28TH NOVEMBER

We hear the odd German and Itie aircraft, but fortunately, no bombs dropped, presumably they're on reconnaissance to see what's going on. I don't mind raids during the day, it's at night when it's worst, everything lights up with flares and you think you see objects moving in the shadows.

FRIDAY 29TH NOVEMBER

Today we are stripping rifles and Browning machine guns for the aircraft. We have been on the go since 8 o'clock this morning. It's our turn to sleep in the armoury on the aerodrome, which is full of live ammunition, so we're hoping for a quiet night! If an enemy bomb should hit it we would end up sitting on the moon!

SATURDAY 30TH NOVEMBER

Pilot Officer Burgess and W/O Lewis are inspecting the armoury, bomb site, surroundings, sand bags and camouflage. We are congratulated for keeping things in good order. It's bloody cold outside.

SUNDAY 1ST DECEMBER

Back in camp, taking things nice and easy. I will definitely be in bed early tonight; these shifts at the aerodrome overnight make me tired.

MONDAY 2ND DECEMBER

8.30am, arrived at the aerodrome, ready for action. Six of our planes took off to escort shipping and join fighters from other squadrons. Our aircraft have been away almost three hours, with long range tanks fitted. They return after four hours, having engaged in combat with Heinkel 3s, four of which were shot down. Among four different fighter squadrons from North Africa, 213 claimed one. At least we are still in the war. Re-armed aircraft, ready for action if needed. Stand down just came through, so relax Jack! Wrote quite a lot of letters home.

TUESDAY 3RD DECEMBER

It seems like years since we came to the Med; it has no end, this bloody senseless war and the weather doesn't help any. Still very cold and now we're wearing khaki battle dress. At last we are preparing for a move to Egypt. Here we go, action stations, five enemy aircraft above and everything's lit up like bonfire night. Heinkel HE3s are dropping bombs on Paphos, St. Jean, Lokatamia and Nicosia.

WEDNESDAY 4TH DECEMBER

Have a 'bath' by improvised methods, using an ammunition box filled with two gallons of hot water, boiled outside my tent. I stand in the box and wash myself down, but unfortunately it is too small for a proper bath. However, I do feel better. In the winter, it's our only means of keeping clean.

THURSDAY 5TH DECEMBER

The antagonism that goes on in these times we are living in seems to have no end. We have just had a lecture telling anyone who is Jewish to remove any means of identification, because if they were caught by the Germans, they would be shot on the spot. We have one or two men in our squadron who are Jewish, and nice fellows they are too. We are on stand-down for two days.

FRIDAY 6TH DECEMBER

I'm certainly 'wrapped up in Cyprus', it's a wonderful place for history. It goes back to the Romans who lived here, and it was said that Sergius Paulus who was Governor of Paphos, was converted to Christianity by St. Paul in AD45. Paphos was the capital of Cyprus in Roman days. I could go on for ever. There are discoveries still to be made. We are on stand-down, so I have to try and write something of interest.

SUNDAY 8TH DECEMBER

Well, Christmas will soon be here. I wonder where we will spend it?

MONDAY 9TH DECEMBER

Some of our squadron have had the privilege of a spot of leave, so I'm heading for Kyrenia, and staying four days at the Dome Hotel. We had our pick of places and I liked this place best. We arrived in time for tea. Before the war the posh folk from all over the world came to this hotel. Aren't I lucky?

TUESDAY 10TH DECEMBER

First class meals all the way. For entertainment at night we play billiards or chess, not that I'm any good, but I have a go, and there are plenty of books to read and walks to be taken. Most of all I have a comfortable bed and a lovely bath or shower, so I'll spoil myself.

WEDNESDAY 11TH DECEMBER

Back to camp. These bloody mosquitoes are a nuisance, they are around from beginning of November until end of December. I have a net over my camp bed at night, otherwise I'm quite comfortable I have felt the benefit of my short leave. I never thought there was a war on, it was so peaceful.

THURSDAY 12TH DECEMBER

We had a collision today, one of our Hurricanes went out of control on landing and hit a lorry. The driver was just bruised slightly. The pilot was a bit shaky, he hit the back of the lorry then carried on and hit a sandbag bay for aircraft. The plane was a write-off. The poor pilot had a right ticking off from the Squadron Leader, but he was made to go up again an hour later, which helps a pilot to get his confidence back... besides we are short of pilots! He took off, had half an hour flying around and landed perfectly. We took the useable parts off the pranged Hurricane and worked till after 9pm.

FRIDAY 13TH DECEMBER

I got the chance to play football for our squadron team, and I played a good game, so I'm 'one of the boys' but a bit painful in the joints at the moment. I thought the Germans and Ities had forgotten us, but no way. Half a dozen Junkers JU88s and four Savoia-Marchetti SM79s. I know because I found a book on enemy aircraft lying about in our armoury months ago. They missed the aerodrome again but they were too close for comfort. Out of trench after five hours.

SATURDAY 14TH DECEMBER

What a horrible war, with all these people trying to kill each other, and for what? The Bible says 'Thou shalt not kill' but nobody seems to listen, least of all the politicians, who are no better than Pontius Pilate who commanded

Jesus to death. We have just been informed to have our bayonets at the ready. The word is that the Germans have parachuted men into the Troodos mountains. Two hours, nothing has happened. There goes the siren, all clear.

SUNDAY 15TH DECEMBER

At times we get false alarms about the enemy trying to penetrate our defences and occupy this island. They have tried almost every military strategy by air, sea and land, but have had no success. I must admit I've had some frightening experiences, especially at the prospect of meeting the enemy face to face with rifle and bayonet. What would be my reaction? I will have to wait and see – it's his life or mine. I do hope it never happens. Even our pilots are armed with pistols and told to use them if necessary. Today, I and two other armourers are on duty at our hut on the aerodrome with fixed bayonets at the ready.

MONDAY 16TH DECEMBER

I think the Germans are making some sort of push because we have to be alert both at camp and aerodrome. The enemy's at their old tricks, dropping booby traps, like pencils, pens, cameras, even fancy rubbers that could be the end of anybody should they play around with them. We have been informed to leave well alone anything we see lying on the ground. I've just come off duty guard, so I'm away to bed until dinner time, I'm half asleep.

TUESDAY 17TH DECEMBER

We have heard of a few casualties in the civilian population. The booby traps that Jerry has dropped have been picked up, even though everyone was cautioned by leaflets throughout the island. Perhaps some may not have got the message in time and it's caused confusion. Fortunately none of our chaps have been hurt. We are still on the alert and ready for an invasion. I pray that it doesn't happen.

WEDNESDAY 18TH DECEMBER

There's been tales about this invasion for a few days. Jerry doesn't know when to stop, up above now are a dozen Junkers JU88s. We scatter in a hurry into trenches because they are dropping small bombs. They can carry up to 360 fragmentation bombs. After they've been released the bomb casings open to form a pair of wings and they spin to the ground like sycamore seeds. The bombs can be fused to detonate on impact or after a pre-set delay, or when disturbed. They are extremely effective aircraft on the ground or soft skinned vehicles. So you know what we are up against. Fortunately we are well sand bagged. There were a few bombs scattered around but no great harm done.

THURSDAY 19TH DECEMBER

The time has come when we may be formed back to a full squadron. Tomorrow we are packing up to fly into Lydda to join the other part of 213 Squadron in Lebanon, just above Haifa. We are now at Nicosia aerodrome checking guns and ammunition, etc. Aircraft are now taking off to fly to Lydda. Some of the squadron will stay back to transport lorries, etc. for embarkation at Famagusta, then on to Tripoli.

FRIDAY 20TH DECEMBER

We are up at 6.30am, breakfast at 7, finished by 8. We are the advance party and now await transport by air by Douglas DC3 Dakota, four of them are waiting on the runway to take us to Lebanon. We take off at 11.30am. We have fighter protection only half way across the Med, then we are on our own – and no parachutes! We are sitting ducks for any enemy fighters out there, which is a bit frightening when you consider the territories we have to fly over. Should our Dakota stray off course or run into a squadron of FW190s it will be 'good bye Jack Walton'! We are greatly relieved to arrive at Lydda aerodrome in one piece after 22 hours in the air. I am so grateful to step on *terra firma* once again that I fall to my knees and I kiss the ground so many times I lose count! Praise the Lord! Halleluja! Amen!

PART THREE

Into The Desert

SATURDAY 21ST DECEMBER

Our accommodation is really bad, in tents, but the grub is great and there is plenty of it. However, it seems we were the only DC3s that took off for Lydda. The others went with some of the squadron ground crew from Paphos, St. Jean's and Larnaca, 203, 73, 127 and 238 Squadrons were at these places. They sometimes came to our base at Nicosia for a refill and then on to the Balkans for raids with 213 Squadron. Fortunately we are staying for two days, then by train from Lydda. It seems there's a shift for all the squadrons and new ones coming out from England will replace us all. Squadrons seem to start on the islands before continuing on to the Western Desert. It's very cold at night, even worse than at home, I'm sleeping in my khaki battle dress, overcoat and socks as well!

SUNDAY 22ND DECEMBER

Lydda seems to be a transit base. We were told to go for our breakfast at 6am, fully clothed and with kit bags packed, ready to move off at 9am. Lorries are ready to transport our convoy to Haifa railway station. When we get there I cannot believe my eyes. I've never seen so many people aboard one train. There are natives on top of the carriages, some even have goats, dogs or hens strapped onto their backs, they hang onto as many items as they can carry. Inside the train, our troops, RAF, Army and Navy, have four carriages. The seats as hard as hell, just slats; and we packed in almost as tightly as the natives, hardly any space left. Even then, as the train starts, more natives jump onto the steps. I've never seen a train loaded like this before. We pass a few native shacks, slums really, then miles and miles of nothing, not even one reasonable building anywhere, poverty no matter where you look. I fall asleep, wake up and have a corned beef sandwich and tea brewed on the train. I keep one eye open and one shut, for the thieving natives.

MONDAY 23RD DECEMBER

We have passed Caesarea, Hadera, Herzliya, and Tel Aviv. I wake up at 7.30am. so I've missed a bit of scenery. The natives are still on top of the train and in between carriages; they must be frozen. We have travelled about 250 to 300 miles down the coast of the Mediterranean. I see glimpses of beautiful greenery, palm trees and sand. My bum is definitely feeling the pinch on these hard seats, and I'll be more than glad when we stop for a toilet, there are none on the train. For breakfast we have hard boiled eggs, biscuits and tea – not exactly living it up! I dream of home, and sitting in a hot bath - aahhh! I'm as stiff as a corpse, still wrapped up in my battledress and overcoat.

TUESDAY 24TH DECEMBER

We are now heading for a place called Ashdod Yam Majda. We arrive two hours late because something was on the rails. Breakfast at 9am. tea brewed on the train, bread and jam. There are no cooking facilities on the train, at the stations traders are selling cooked food, but we have been told not to buy any because these natives cook in such dirty conditions that it could cause illness. God knows when we will have our next good meal! At Gaza the train stops to let troops go to the toilet, but the toilets are in such a terrible state, we are given a spade and told to dig our own pit. I was bursting, so I dug! What a war but what a relief! The train's on its way again, passing Khan Yunus; the next station is El Arish. It's now dark and cold, I'm still sleeping in battledress, overcoat and boots.

WEDNESDAY 25TH DECEMBER

What a way to spend Christmas day, travelling on a trains made in Victorian times, with hard seats, open windows and no toilets. We are now leaving the coast and heading inland, a little greenery, then sand and sand. We head for Romani, then on to Qantara East, Firdar and Ismailia, where we stop for a breather - 4 hours. As soon as one lot of natives get off another lot swarm like bees all over the train with all their belongings - chickens, goats, calves, whatever they can carry. We are off again, Tel el Kàbir, Zigazig, Benha, Qajab, finally we are almost at our destination.

Here we are at Cairo, near a place called Sida Garbo. We must have travelled well over a thousand miles and my arse is very sore due to these bloody wooden seats! We are staying here for the night then moving on tomorrow, in lorries, up towards Alexandria.

THURSDAY 26TH DECEMBER

Up at 6am, breakfast at 7am, a very good feed indeed, better than 'corned dog' and biscuits we had on our way here. Left Sida Garbo at 8.30am, passing Giza an hour and a half later, coming to a place called Ashmur. All I've seen is sand but here is a small oasis. We stop and have a brew and some grub. The natives want to sell us eggs and all kinds of fruit - even goats and pigs! You wouldn't think there was a war on. Heading now for Hinuf – nothing but sand everywhere. Making for a place called Shibingi Kom. Stopped at Kafr-ez-Zarvet, another oasis, slightly larger

We enjoy a late Christmas dinner in the desert.

than the last one. It seems like a market place for camels and all sorts of things, a trading post, very busy, lots of natives with camel trains. We brew up again, stay for half an hour for toilet necessities (spade job again), and are on our way once more, passing a place called Mahalla-al-Kibra, another trading post.

Away into the barren land again to a place called Disuq, then passing by Abu-Harrius and finally our destination - Idku. We are told that the camp is not ready. We stay on the lorries and are taken to Abu Qir, fortunately it only takes 20 minutes to get there. We arrive at 7pm, and what a nice surprise they have put on for us. Knowing we had missed our Christmas dinner it is all laid on for us. Boy, what a feed! Nothing missed out, and 30 of us enjoy every minute. There are still quite a few of our squadron lads and equipment left on Cyprus and six aircraft, but they are following on. I feel very tired, especially after the drink – but we certainly didn't expect this party!

FRIDAY 27TH DECEMBER

This transit camp at Abu Qir is quite a change from our last few days of travelling without ever taking our uniforms, socks or boots off. I can't believe it, we have a great opportunity of luxury, of soaking in hot water, a real bath, and afterwards a good supper, then off to bed with clean sheets. Before you can appreciate simple luxuries, you have to rough it for a while. I'm looking forward to a good night's sleep. I would like to stay for a while but unfortunately we'll be on the move again shortly. There's a bit of history here; Cleopatra's dwellings and the remains of a Pharaoh's palace; also there was a battle between Nelson's fleet and the Egyptians. There are the remains of some cannons from the sunken boats lying on the beach.

SATURDAY 28TH DECEMBER

After a bit of a lie in, had breakfast at 9am. What a change to sit at tables with cloths, and natives serving. We have just been told that on 24th August, 1941 *HMS Barrum* was sunk, and attempts were made on other ships in Alexandria harbour. Our frogmen were alerted and disengaged mines from our ships and we believe that two or three German frogmen were shot and killed. It seems like there's a lot of activity near the western desert, so maybe our next move is nearer to the action, which our squadron is looking forward to. We are expecting a move tomorrow to Idku. Maybe there could be another delay, however, I don't mind staying here, it's like being on holiday, we are even going to a cinema. Enjoyed picture. In bed by 11pm.

SUNDAY 29TH DECEMBER

Arrived at breakfast 9am, natives serving out meals, porridge, eggs, beans, sausage. We have been told that we can visit Alexandria for the day, so my pals and I arrive in the city, have a look around, have tea in Egyptian cafe (steak, peas, carrots, cabbage, as good as any in England). I must say that the journey by train from Lebanon, through Israel and Egypt by coast, then inland to Cairo and on to Alexandria was a fantastic eye-full of Egyptian and Arabic history. All those thousands of years and still standing: statues of gods, monuments of worship, pyramids, aqueducts, which we'd never seen the likes of anywhere in our travels in England. Those Pharaoh's could teach our lot a thing or two about building construction. Most of the statues amazed me, such huge figures, bigger than any I have seen, and the irrigation systems, still working with same methods as thousands of years ago. The temples such as temple of Rameses III at Medinet Habou, covered with inscriptions relating to victories of the king over Egypt's enemies. Temple of Kourna, built by King Sethos I and dedicated to Amon-Ra. Rock tomb of Pharaohs in the famous valley of the Kings at Thebes and the colossal statue of Rameses at Deir-el-Behari and inscribed at the bottom 'Theg' which means a very high position over all the Egyptians. I could go on for ever!

MONDAY 30TH DECEMBER

Up early for a move to El-Amiriya, finished breakfast, all into lorries and ready for our destination quite a few miles from Abu Qir. Arrived 2.30pm, nothing but sand, sand, sand, it is right on the edge of the Western Desert. We are expected just to stay for a few days to re-form and ready for action. We are hit by a sandstorm, our first experience of one and we are taught the art of survival on such occasions. It's very easy to get lost, we have been told – so always stay where you are, sit down, and use any materials to make sure your eyes and mouth are covered, and if possible, your whole body. Make a hole in the sand to cover yourself, wait and be patient, even if it last hours.

At last it dies down. I'm absolutely covered in sand. We are on the move to Idku tomorrow.

TUESDAY 31ST DECEMBER

What a day to move, New Year's Eve, 9.30am and away we go, destination Idku. When leaving El-Amiriya, looking out of the tent, my thoughts were "What a hell of a place to die in!" I wouldn't mind if there were trees, grass, greenery of any kind, but sand, thousands of miles of noting else. Let's hope the Lord's on my side. However, we travelled from El-Amiriya north to a village, Mex, right on the coast, heading back to Abu Qir; 14 MU are based just on the outskirts of Alexandria. Then we are on our

A desert sandstorm.

way to Lake Idku, our destination. Joyfully we discover that there are trees and grass. It seems the runway is flat sand and as good as any surface. Unpacking our equipment, we pitch tents for sleeping accommodation. We have a marquee with space for 14 of us inside, our home for the time being. Fortunately I made myself a camp bed, the others sleep on cane beds and mattresses. Seemingly the big hut on camp serves as the cookhouse and stores, etc. Idku has a very small population of Arabs who live outside this makeshift aerodrome. We are pestered by salesmen, selling eggs, fruit, tins of everything, including sweets, chocolate, nuts – you name it, they've got it. Believe me, they won't go unless you buy something, but our military police scarpered them pretty quickly! Teatime, thank God, we've a proper place to dine with tables and forms, and cooks dishing out in a proper style, real good meals, and a pleasant change from corned beef and biscuits.

NEW YEAR WEDNESDAY 1ST JANUARY, 1942

One thing about our camp, we are not far from a town, Idku, seems more or less like an oasis and has a lake. We see plenty of Arab fishermen sailing on the lake with huge fabrics on their boats. It's a popular place for Arabs, known as 'wogs' by all RAF bods. They are dressed in gowns like nightshirts (nothing underneath so they tell me, no vest or pants), and small round hats patterned like crochet. Their houses are not very well constructed, made from blocks of clay and camel dung, with small rooms. On cold nights they have a fire on the floor in the middle of the building, and the smoke rises through a hole in the flat roof. It is remarkable they withstand all weathers. Most are painted inside and out with some kind of white stuff, it has a hell of a smell! When it's dry it looks very clean. The natives too have a peculiar smell; some are allowed into camp, two or three work in the cookhouse and the doctor's Nissen hut doing odd jobs, such as emptying toilet buckets, most of which are taken to use on their small plantations as fertiliser. They also get all the scraps from the cookhouse. I must admit they certainly have shifty eyes, they never miss a thing, even what we throw out of our tents, everything goes into their bags, nothing's missed. I sometimes wonder if they are eyeing things up to be 'knocked off', although I don't suppose they would, especially when they would lose their permits to be on camp.

THURSDAY 2ND JANUARY 1942

Up early, 6.30, our first patrol starts 9.30, so most ground crew are on the aerodrome. Six of our Hurricanes are on their way to join up with Blenheims escorting for submarine bombing and shipping in the Mediterranean. We hear that the Germans are pushing large amounts of men and military equipment into their bases around North Africa, which means they are building up for a big push, but we don't know when or where it will be.

We are all on edge, waiting for the return of our six aircraft, but at last, after what seems an eternity, they're back, all returning with no damage, not even to the Blenheims. They dropped their bombs on suspect images, three submarines. Our Hurricanes flew down to confirm, oil patches were seen. I must say these pilots are worthy of praise in the highest, no matter what 'plane they fly.

Like most good things we now have a real canteen, part of the cookhouse. There's radio and you can buy anything in the way of eats, but best of all, electric light, charged by a generator outside, well cased in with bolts cemented into the ground to stop the natives pilfering. At night we entertain ourselves with a sing-song, and at times our pilots join in. I sleep better now after having a good pint of best and a little brandy, so it's good night all!

FRIDAY 3RD JANUARY

Our squadron's having a spell of leave, so two of my mates and I have four days, our accommodation is what you would call in England, a very big mansion, which now is used by all the Forces. It runs under the name of the Alexandria Fleet Club. The ballroom is very large, that's where we sleep. We pay for mattress and blankets, and during the day we have meals out. We are now on our way to tram station and then on for a swim, believe it or not it's one shilling for a lock-up cubicle. By tram it only takes 10 or 15 minutes up this lovely bay, called Stanley Bay, what a place for a swim, and there's a small cafe selling anything you want.

Two of the RAF fellows were telling us about the Greeks and Turks causing a bit of friction in Alexandria. I remember before leaving camp that the Greek and Turkish quarters were out of bounds. I thought it funny before we got our keys, they asked for a look at our pay book.

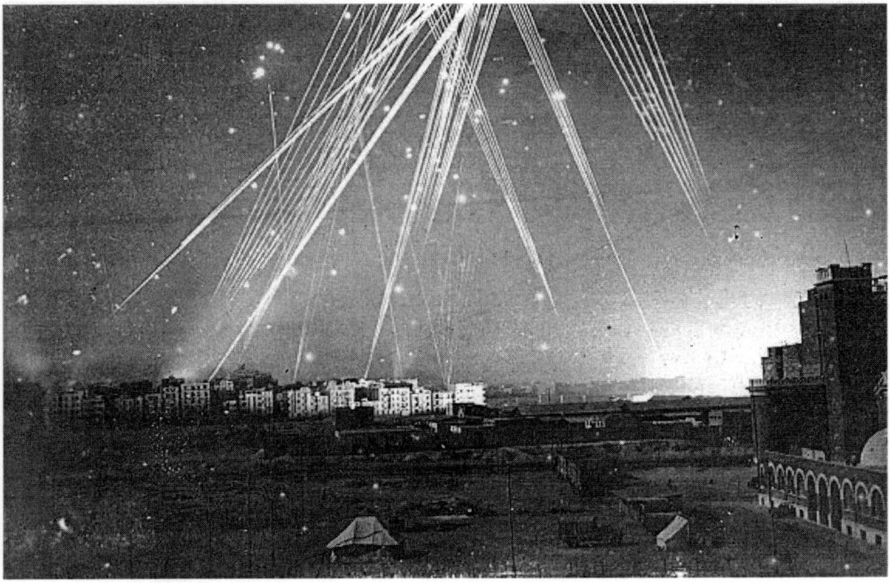

'Fireworks' over Alexandria (above) and Tripoli (below).

Believe it or not, Egyptian police stopped and asked me for my identification as he said that I looked like a Greek because I was suntanned with black hair. Of course my two pals verified me. You could almost say I was as black as the Egyptian policeman who questioned me! After we left him we made our way to a skating rink and ended the evening jubilantly. Arrived back at the Fleet Club ready for bed, 12.30 a.m.

SATURDAY 4TH JANUARY

We are up like the larks. Six of our Hurricanes are escorting some Douglas A-20B 'Bostons' that have come down from the edge of the Western Desert – they are big, carrying more bombs than even Blenheims. Our Hurricanes carry small bombs also, four of them. They are targeting enemy shipping from Crete, where, for months, reconnaissance planes have been taking photographs showing that the Germans are ready to move tanks, lorries, heavy flak and ammunition to parts of North Africa. 213 Squadron's Hurricanes are fitted with long range tanks that can keep them in the air approximately four or five hours, so we have a long wait to find out if they all return safely. They do… 3½ hours later. It's a nerve racking time, the waiting.

SUNDAY 5TH JANUARY

You won't believe this. At 5am, instead of waking up to see the inside of our marquee, I am looking up at the stars and sky. Some of the other lads are still sleeping but come to life and wonder what the hell is going on. The Arabs

The author with fellow ground-crew pals (above) and with one of the Hurricanes he was responsible for arming (below).

have stolen it! A 20ft by 20ft marquee tent has disappeared into thin air with 14 blokes sleeping in it! They even took the poles and pegs. I've just heard they nicked another of the same type, and four kitbags – and no one even saw them! At 11 a.m. four Egyptian policemen and two of our own police with 30 airmen went to three villages outside aerodrome searching houses, but with no success. One of the Egyptian policemen said that the thieves had possibly travelled some distance. The tents would probably be used to make sails for fishing boats, so, when our pilots observing from the sky look down and see sails that look like tents, they belong to 213 Squadron! The Egyptians who stole the tents certainly had a good night. After six hours the search was called off. What a joke! Talk about sleeping beauties!

MONDAY 6TH JANUARY

Received a letter from Mrs Wilson from Durban telling us that some of the people from the Scottish church in Durban have written and sent parcels to England filled with all sorts of items that are hard to get there at the moment. Mail from the UK is still bad, it sometimes takes three or four months, then we get a pile if we're lucky. Our squadron is on stand-down for a few days. After the incident with the tents we are expecting the arrival of a detachment of the RAF Regiment to guard our camp and aircraft. For the moment the ground crews will have to take turns to do guard duties, as well as their usual duties, which is going to be tiresome. Let's hope they don't take too long in getting here.

TUESDAY 7TH JANUARY

Still no trace of our tents. We have travelled to collect ammunition, small bombs, etc for our aircraft and other military equipment from a supply depot at Khakan, just outside Cairo. There is nothing here but sand. Along with Flt/Lt Holmes, our armament officer we are security guards. He is armed with a pistol and six of us have Italian rifles at the ready in case they are needed. We stay for the night, sleeping on cane beds with straw 'biscuits' and blankets, not bad really, and the grub's good, they have a canteen, a wooden building. Our Italian rifles were captured when they surrendered at Derna. About 1,000 Italians decided to pack it in, they had had enough. One of the Durham Light Infantry lads said that they were glad because they didn't want to fight and didn't mind being prisoners of war – at least they'll be alive when it ends. Some lads who've been in the Western Desert since the war started, from 73, 32, 238, 237 and 32 Squadrons have come to where we are for rest and recuperation. They have told some horror stories of the desert war during General Wavell and General Cunningham's command. Men with their heads blown off, no arms or legs and flies eating at bodies. I'm not looking forward to our move when the time comes for the push. Better make the most of our situation now. I'm having a pint or two! Cheers!

WEDNESDAY 8TH JANUARY

Apparently the Air Ministry is siphoning-off Hurricanes and other supplies to go to the Far East. Number 30 Squadron has been ordered to Ceylon to patrol the

Mediterranean. According to our pilots, Rommel's forces are back to the El-Gazala/Bir Hakim defence line. A Hurricane pilot of No.4 SAAF Squadron confirmed that an Axis advance is imminent. He reports that Italian troops are moving towards the Allied positions near El Gazala. Three German divisions are also involved and a battle for Bir Hakim, held by the Free French has raged for 10 days. The French brigade withstood the sustained assault due to assistance received from RAF fighters, who decided to 'adopt' the Free French and their 'fortress'. Hurricanes helped to fight off Luftwaffe attacks, dropped supply canisters, and the new Hurricane IID tank busters of No. 6 Squadron, tore into Rommel's armour. The determination of No. 6 Squadron, in pressing home their attacks, was an example to us all. Good show!

One of 213 Squadron's Hurricanes in the Western Desert.

THURSDAY 9TH JANUARY

Four of our aircraft are on loan for front line and reconnaissance patrols over Crete and our convoys in the Med for a week or so, then back to Idku. Until now we have not lost any planes or pilots. When our aircraft land up towards front line for refuelling for their return leg, pilots from the other squadrons tell them what's going on, so we are never without news. The Axis advance at Bir Hakim has slowed and the Eighth Army has been pushed into an 800-mile retreat to El Alamein, its last line of defence before Cairo.

FRIDAY 10TH JANUARY

At the moment tranquillity surrounds us at this aerodrome, without that feeling that maybe we are just waiting to die. We are quite a long way from Rommel's advance here. On stand-by for 24 hours. Two German Dornier 17-P-3(F)22's on a reconnaissance mission, drop flares to try and pick out two squadrons on Idku aerodrome without any success because we are definitely well up-to-date with our camouflage nets. No wonder they call Rommel called 'the desert fox', he seems to know everything that's going on.

SATURDAY 11TH JANUARY

It's a hard task for ships to supply us with new aircraft via the Mediterranean, with it being full of German subs. They decided to send a convoy by a new route from the north of Ireland towards the coast of North America almost to Newfoundland. It was then escorted by the American Navy down to South America then across the Atlantic to Takoradi on the West coast of Africa. The cargo of Hurricanes and Spitfires in crates was unloaded, they were reassembled at Takoradi then flown over safe zones in Africa to aerodromes in Egypt and Libya. It was a very big convoy from England and there are more planes to come. It seems obvious that something big is coming off.

SUNDAY 12TH JANUARY

Our squadron's aircraft are still patrolling in the Mediterranean, where the Italian Air Force (the Regia Aeronautica) have been busy. They are not as well equipped as Rommel's Luftwaffe and the Italian fighters are not as good as our Hurricanes. One of our pilots kept his eyes open and followed a Heinkel III that had become separated from the others and shot it down. The crew of four baled out of the Heinkel but one parachute didn't open. Two were captured soon after they landed. The last crew member was missing for a time until it was found that he had parachuted into the sea, freed himself from his harness and swum ashore; he was captured on the beach and taken prisoner. It was one of our Sergeant Pilots who had all the glory – he had only just joined the squadron and it was only his second operational flight! Good show!

MONDAY 13TH JANUARY

It seems that our squadron is on stand-by. We had been about to move to the edge of the Western Desert, then it was cancelled. We are to stay put at Idku until further notice. Apparently, our Generals cannot get the equipment they want, partly because since the Japanese declared war in the Far East we have had to divert men and supplies out there. Auchinleck has been up and down the desert so many times, advancing and retreating, it's hard to tell when things will get better. It's a hard task he's got, I would not like his job.

TUESDAY 14TH JANUARY

I have a day off. I'm inside the tent, it's too hot outside. Looking out from inside the tent, all I can see are a few palm trees and flat sand. I'm very homesick at the moment. How I wish someone with a magic wand would send me home, even just for a little while...

WEDNESDAY 15TH JANUARY

A squadron of Blenheim MkIV-42's and a squadron of Beaufighters from the desert are helping our squadron patrol in the Mediterranean, protecting our convoys and attacking German shipping and aircraft, so now we can expect a few visits from enemy aircraft. Just finished checking up on guns, now on stand-by ready for tomorrow's operation.

THURSDAY 16TH JANUARY

Beaufighters of 272 Squadron did most of their operations along with ours, more so than the Blenheim squadron. They patrol edge of Western Desert, refuel and land on some aerodrome whenever necessary. Rumours are that the reason Rommel has ordered so much equipment is because he's intending to push the Eighth Army right back, to capture Egypt. So all squadrons round about are fairly busy, quite a few from landing grounds between Alexandria and Cairo. It's said he's very determined, also there's a possibility he may use parachutists. Our squadron, along with the Beaufighters, have noticed quite a lot of shipping coming from Crete and then on to Tobruk. Today, when patrolling the Mediterranean, they dropped their bombs on a convoy and strafed, but nothing confirmed. However, they all returned safely. Pilots said damage was done to ships. We are now re-arming our guns, ready for action. In bed, fully clothed, ready for any German parachutists, with rifle and bayonet at bedside!

FRIDAY 17TH JANUARY

Our squadron orders from RAF Command are to proceed to have all aircraft checked and re-checked, also equipment that each aircraft requires, ammunition for all weapons, explosives, pyrotechnics etc. From today until 31st January we are on stand-by, all leave cancelled. But orders from Cairo are to stay put at Idku. These days everything seems to be one way - retreat, and we are standing still. We have had one or two Hurricane squadrons from the desert front line staying for a few days, and pilots tell of slaughtered bodies, camels and goats laid out in the desert for miles and miles, pitiful sights to see.

A 'pep-talk' from Lord Trenchard.

Churchill, King George V and General Montgomery inspecting the troops in the Middle East, 1942.

18TH JANUARY TO 27TH FEBRUARY

Our squadron's a lame duck stuck in Idku. We are all packed and ready to participate in any emergency as soon as word comes. It will be a relief to be ready for the big show.

MONDAY 28TH FEBRUARY, 1942

We are allowed leave to go into Alexandria, I will certainly take advantage, and why not?

SATURDAY 5TH MARCH

Went on leave to Alexandria for 24 hours. Left camp 5 o'clock, arrived in Alex 6.30pm. Booked a mattress at Fleet Club for service personnel before boarding the tram to Stanley Bay skating rink. Enjoyable night – until disembarking from tram - I was followed and knocked unconscious, I woke up in hospital five hours later with a broken nose, headache, with pay book and wallet missing. Had it not been for a Military Policeman it could have been worse, at least I survived!

SATURDAY 12TH MARCH

Dismissed from hospital, report back to Squadron, inform our MO on camp, who examines my nose, finds it has been broken but nothing has been done to fix it and sends me back to the hospital.

TUESDAY 15TH MARCH

Go to hospital to see surgeon who examines my nose and tells me there is nothing more he can do, as have no permanent damage and can breathe normally. I proceed back to camp at Idku. When I arrive, picking up a newspaper, I am astonished to see that *HMS Exeter* is missing. She came out with our convoy when I was on the *Georgic*.

THURSDAY 22ND APRIL

I am missing a lot of dates because there is nothing much to say, just the same old routines. Today the Duke of Gloucester is arriving to give us a 'talk', which, no doubt, will be the same old bullshit we have heard so many times before. Thank God he's gone, it's plain to see he won't be sleeping in a flea-bitten bed like we are. They should have sent him up the 'blue' (desert) for a year or two to get the sandfly blues (shits)!

We have had a Jerry or two dropping bombs over Alexandria, Saint Andrew's Hostel was hit, also the harbour. We heard over the wireless that seven of the enemy were shot down by 213 Squadron and 272 Squadron's Beaufighters. One of our pilots followed a plane down, the German baled out, was caught in a short time and taken prisoner.

SATURDAY 30TH MAY

At last our squadron is to participate in the Western Desert. It's almost a year we've had to wait. Left Idku today for operations with Army in Egypt and Libya. Time of leaving 10.30 a.m. Bombed and strafed by a Heinkel HEM, armed with a remote controlled gun in the tail, tracers firing everywhere, we all dispersed from lorries, we couldn't get off quick enough! Sheltered in ditches alongside the road, what a greeting for our first visit! Fortunately none of convoy was damaged. We camped off Tuka, a bit off the road, camouflaged the lorries and slept underneath and believe me it was bloody cold! Put groundsheet, blanket underneath me, then kept everything on, including boots, then covered up for the night. On our way up there was debris all over the place and many makeshift graveyards with crosses.

SUNDAY 31ST MAY

We are ready to move forward to our next destination, Cita Nish. Pitched tents. We arrived here at 4pm. I must say, what a desolate place! We are well off the coast, nothing but sand, sand, sand, as far as we can see. I'm so tired after that journey, I'm into my bivouac to settled down for the night.

THURSDAY 4TH JUNE

What bloody awful weather, words cannot describe it, the changes, red hot and unbearable, sand storms, impossible to work. During the night it's even colder than an icy winter back home; I sleep with my clothes on, apart from my boots. I'm really glad when morning comes. After staying here for four days we're on the move again. A pep talk on booby traps, whatever you see, leave well alone and just forget it, the Germans like leaving surprises, so be on your guard. On our way back to the aerodrome we are travelling in the back of lorry, full of our own importance, when a bloody Junkers 88 strafes our convoy. We lie in the ditch, luckily we chose this particular side, otherwise we may have been shot to bits! One or two of the lorries are hit, but no serious damage or casualties and we carry on to our destination.

FRIDAY 5TH JUNE

We arrive at our new destination, Gambut West LG3 aerodrome, pitch tents and bivouac at 4.30pm, feeling bloody tired and worn out after three long journeys. It seems this will now be our base for a while, but what a place, right on top of a flat hill, which stretches for miles and miles, nothing but sand, not even a weed or blade of grass. How I long for home!

Would you believe it, a sandstorm has blown up just when we are about to have tea. I cover it with a towel until I get back to my bivouac. Not very comfortable but I manage, just. On the way here we passed Mersah Matruh, Sidi Barani, Halfaya Pass, Sollum and Bardia. How dangerous those passes are, one slip and over you go, nothing to stop you, then one big drop and its curtains. Thank God for our fighters, which were patrolling overhead; we would have been easy targets, believe me. We were a very big convoy.

I can hear the sound of big guns. There is a tank battle going on about 30 miles away at Bir El Hachem. The

Germans have just captured the aerodrome – they are too close for my liking!

SATURDAY 6TH JUNE

Things are looking bad. If we have to evacuate in a hurry we will have to leave the ammunition dump. Fortunately, we dug a hell of a big hole and that will have been covered with sand. Maybe if we return we can find it again – if the Germans don't find it first... Here comes trouble, a Messerschmitt BF109 flying very low. We jump into trenches. Bombs are going off and tracers are bouncing all over the place. Our pilots have been battling with the ME109s and say they seem to be a little faster than our Hurricanes, but not as manoeuvrable.

It seems there's still a heavy tank battle at Bir Hacheim and word has just come for us to pack up, we are on the retreat, not even time to have tea. We have never moved so fast! We are departing now from Gambut West.

7TH TO 15TH JUNE

It turns out we were fortunate to leave Gambut, because the Germans blasted the hell out of it and now occupy the landing ground. During the past 10 days we have no sooner settled down than word has come to be on the move again, quickly. We have camped at Halfaya LG79, then Bug-Bug LG97. Stayed a few days then our destination was Sidi Barani. We turned right-out of town onto a sandy road, nothing else but barren land, took almost an hour to reach LG76.

Our convoy is strafed and anti-personnel bombs are dropped, (when dropped, these weapons fly and disperse over a wide area). When the attack begins we all jump off our lorry and scatter in different directions, hurling ourselves flat on the deck. When the attack is over we hear someone shouting to us.

"Whatever you do, don't try to move!"

Four of us have unwittingly run into a minefield! We spend two-and-a-half agonising hours lying still until an Army bomb disposal squad arrives. The sappers form a line with their detectors and when they get to us they have to probe under our bodies - very, very carefully – a bit of a job. At last the four of us got up, lathered in sweat, even though it was only 6.30am. The sappers then used their detectors to see where the minefield started and told us that if we had gone another six feet, the four of us would have been blown to pieces by anti-tank mines. I was never so glad to be on that lorry and on our way. The attack set fire to four lorries and killed 10 army lads.

TUESDAY 16TH JUNE

We are at LG155 (Sida Omar).

WEDNESDAY 17TH JUNE

Sidi Barani, LG75. We hear that the poor infantry at Tobruk have been cut off. The Germans formed a pincer movement and their navy bombarded from outside the harbour. Some of the infantry who escaped from Tobruk re-formed in our convoy. They told us that before the

Germans took over there were so many bodies they hadn't time to dig graves, so the infantry dug a large hole where they laid them to rest and poured gallons of petrol over them and set fire to them. Time was running out and they had no other option, rather than let the wild animals get at them. Some of the infantry lads in our convoy had helped with the digging and the cremation; they said the smell was horrible. What the hell is it all for? All because of that madman Hitler.

20TH – 26TH JUNE

On the move from LG76 near Sidi Barani. It's amazing, the DAF (Desert Air Force) is composed of literally every Allied nationality taking part in the war. Such a conglomeration of languages, creeds and widely different backgrounds, but they all get on astonishingly well in the desert 'team'. With a sense of unreality, I am watching history being made in this wilderness of rock and sand, a place only fit for war.

At night enemy air activity seems to be minimal, but is still effective. Rommel and his Panzer divisions are forcing us to retreat. If they keep this performance up Alexandria will be captured in a short time and we could all become a prisoners of war. There's no doubting Rommel's had success from the start. We retreat to LG155 (Gita Nish), then LG7 where we're going to stay. Unfortunately Rommel doesn't give up so we move on to LG154. Still on move, a short stay at LG12 near Mersa Matruh.

SATURDAY 27TH JUNE

We finish up at El Daba, pitch our bivouacs, have tea, and are just ready for a kip when German aircraft pay us a visit and strafe the aerodrome, dropping bombs. The raid lasts for almost two hours. We had Army ack-ack around, fortunately, so the planes didn't do much damage. We are told to sleep in our khaki battledress in case we need to make a quick getaway. Lorries are kept loaded. We dig trenches, put our bivouacs over the top and sleep on the hard ground with the usual ground sheets and blankets and wearing overcoat and boots. Just as well as it's bloody cold and it won't get any warmer. Aircraft and lorries are covered with nets in sand colours. We are quite a few miles from the front line, but what a hell of a noise, all kinds of guns going, ours and the Germans', sleep is impossible, we can see from our tents flare after flare lighting up the sky, just like Blackpool illuminations. Oh, for a peaceful night's sleep! It sounds like there are Heinkel IIIs about, the type that have a remote-controlled gun in the tail. When they get a chance to strike, you need to dive right into a trench, because tracer bullets spray in different directions, from the top, underneath, front and sides of the plane. They're also packed with bombs. Six of them flew right over our landing ground without seeing us – you can't beat a good bit of camouflage!

TUESDAY 30TH JUNE

We had to moved from El Daba aerodrome fast. Fortunately everybody was sleeping fully clothed, ready for the off. We had hardly been five minutes on the lorry when we had to make a dash for cover. German Messerschmitt BF109s, six of them, strafed and bombed the convoy. Ten Army personnel were killed, but luckily no RAF. I've never seen a convoy like it, miles and miles, we are sitting ducks! We proceed two or three miles more and then suddenly there is a huge explosion. From out of nowhere, a group of Junkers JU87s appears, strafing and dropping bombs. We all jump off the lorries and make for some rocks near the side of the road. We are half way there when there is another loud bang. The convoy has been hit with quite a lot of casualties. The blast wave hits me and nearly knocks the life out of me. In what seems like the next minute I find myself confronted by my Warrant Officer, pointing a pistol at me and saying that I will be court martialled if I don't get back to the convoy. It seems that three of my mates tried to get me back to the trucks but I couldn't move, no matter what they did. I must have been in that condition, rigid with fear, for about 12 hours. Eventually my W/O and two mates manage to bring me back to the convoy and I cannot remember a anything properly. I am in a state of shock, but I come around to my old self a few hours later and the W/O apologises about the incident with the pistol. He knew I was just too frightened to move.

31ST JUNE TO 1ST JULY

A short stay at LG154 near El Alamein, then on to LG145 at Amriya. We dig new accommodations in the sand with a roof to safeguard us from flying shrapnel. It looks like we're staying for a while. Our aircraft have been bombing and strafing enemy targets. Now Jerry has started dropping

Corporal Wilbur Wright paints the Squadon crest on one of the aircraft in the Western Desert.

A bit of a prang. A Hurricane and a Wellington collide in wet conditions at Mera Tuaba LG2 in 1941.

flares but we are well camouflaged, no bombs dropped on us, but the South African Squadron's landing strip gets well blasted. There was quite a bit of damage but none on our LG. We stay here almost three weeks, but we are moving to another LG up near the front line!

WEDNESDAY 23RD JULY

Moved back to LG172. We arrive at 2200 hours at Burg-El-Arab, flares dropping all over the place. We are about 12 miles from our last aerodrome. It's like daylight due to the flares. Fortunately our aircraft are not arriving until tomorrow for daylight raids on tanks, aerodromes, convoys and ammunition dumps. Right now, tracers from our ack-ack guns are going full blast and non-stop. We pitch our bivouacs after digging in. God knows what it will be like when our aircraft arrive!

FRIDAY 25TH JULY

Our aircraft were supposed to arrive yesterday but don't show up until 9 o'clock at night. We have to improvise landing lights and put them out quickly. Something's wrong! The planes taxi right towards our bivouacs and one of them rolls over somebody's tent One of our lads, Turnbull, is killed instantly. How upset everybody is.

SATURDAY 26TH JULY

We retreat to LG154 for the next two days. Our RAF Regiment holds a funeral for young Turnbull at El-Alamein.

A lone ME110 shot down in the desert (above) and a group of them abandoned by retreating German forces (below).

The poor lad is buried in blankets, he belonged to the RAF Regiment. How sad everybody is today, and there is more bad news, six of our aircraft took off and were on their way to the front line, but after only a quarter of an hour in the air some Messerschmitt BF109s came out of the sun and our pilots didn't see them swooping down and were knocked out of the sky. Perhaps if our Hurricanes were fitted with mirrors, like the ME109s, things might have been different. Two pilots were killed, two force landed, two baled out. The two pilots had only been with the squadron for just a few days when they were killed, the other four had joined us earlier.

Rommel is almost on the doorstep, not a long way from Alexandria or Cairo. From our aerodrome we can hear plenty of action, guns and more guns, firing on both sides. Sleep is impossible.

MONDAY 28TH JULY

We are on our way back to LG145. Rommel on the advance. We leave at 10.15am and arrive at 12.45am. We just take ground sheets and blankets off the lorry, spread them on the ground and sleep in the open air with uniforms and top coats on. I covered my head with blanket, boy it's hellishly cold! 61 times I've done this since entering the desert, without assembling a bivouac. We are told we'll be on the move any time, because of the retreat. I'm bloody sick of this stinking war!

WEDNESDAY 30TH JULY

Left LG145 at Amriya at 2pm, arrived at Heliopolis near Cairo 8pm. Pitched our bivouacs, in bed by 9pm, dog tired, sick of eating corned dog.

THURSDAY 31ST JULY

What a change, especially the food, no 'corned dog', really good food. At night there's a canteen, you can have a good supper for 10/- if you've missed the one in camp.

TUESDAY 19TH AUGUST

I went to Cairo with a couple of mates, visited the Pyramids, temples, the Sphinx, took photographs, came back into Cairo. We had tea, then off to the pictures. What a posh place! The day went marvellously, back to camp 10.40pm, in bed by 11pm. An experience of a lifetime. Before the war people paid a lot of money to come here - we paid nothing!

SATURDAY 23RD AUGUST

Now that we've had a good rest, enjoying every minute, we're proceeding back into the hell of the Western Desert, arriving at LG85, El Amriya. Same thing as usual, we dig in, make a trench big enough, fortunately I have a luxury camp bed I made, now finished digging, placing bivouac over my little home 6ft x 4ft x 2ft6, then built up sand banks around tent, protection from shrapnel and anti-personnel bombs. We are still organised camouflaging

Armoured vehicles abandoned in haste by Rommel's defeated forces.

the aircraft, we have dummy ones, which the army erect away from our squadron. Not far from here El Hamman, a temporary port for supplies, was heavily bombed, we saw enemy aircraft dropping flares. Two Junkers 88s were shot down by a squadron based at Idku, behind front line, about 30 miles away.

31ST AUGUST TO 10TH SEPTEMBER

This past week we have had raid after raid. Night after night enemy aircraft are dropping flares and bombs. They know we are building up our forces and they are not giving us any rest. Our anti-aircraft guns have shot down three Italian fighters, Maachi MC2s, Italy's most up-to-date aircraft. Six aircraft of A Flight took off to strafe Rommel's airfields and ammunition dumps or anything else they can see of his military equipment. They return after two hours and taxi into bays. 'My' aircraft – 'H' for Harry – shot down three Junkers 87s. The pilot is pleased, all four cannons fired extremely well, he was full of praise, after all, his life depends on those cannon. I re-arm guns, ready for next operation. This time our six aircraft bagged 10 lorries, three enemy aircraft in the air and four on the ground, not bad at all! But what a bloody war, trying to kill each other!

British air power seems to have had an effect on Rommel's Panzer divisions. He's having a bit of a lull and we seem to be keeping him at bay.

Suddenly there is a screaming noise and out of the sun come a squadron of Stukas. We hurl ourselves to the ground and try to take cover, bombs bursting all around us. Fortunately the barrage from the Army anti-aircraft guns

Tobruk harbour in 1942 (above) full of sunken ships of every kind.
A panoramic view from the Sollum Pass (below)

knocks six of them right out of the sky. I'm glad, good riddance!

We stay here for quite a while, even though the enemy pays us a lot of visits, day and night. Thank God for our camouflaged netting and dummy aircraft!

WEDNESDAY 10TH SEPTEMBER

Douglas A20Bs 'Bostons' have arrived over at the other side of the airfield, this could be part of the build-up for a big push. It also means we can expect to be regularly visited by enemy aircraft at night. The Bostons seem to be revving up at full throttle for a mission, probably to bomb enemy shipping in the Mediterranean. Six of our Hurricanes escort them.

Oh no, here come those bloody Stukas again, full blast, dropping bombs but as usual, missing the target. I'm tucked up in my little trench home, but even so when those Stukas come diving down with their sirens screaming it is very frightening, I've never experienced anything like it anywhere. Fortunately enemy aircraft are having a hell of a time trying to locate targets because of the camouflage. Thank God, the all-clear sounds and I can stretch my legs.

TUESDAY 30TH SEPTEMBER

Still at LG85, still plenty of action at our long stay near the front line. We certainly have had plenty of enemy aircraft over and many exciting moments jumping in and out of trenches. There is another kind of enemy too – sandstorms, you can't see a thing in-front of you. When we go to the

Pilots and ground crew of 213 Squadron with a Hawker Hurricane. (Author second row, third from left.)

South African AF Douglas A20B Boston on duty in the Desert War.

cookhouse there's more sand on the plate than the meal, no wonder we have-the 'pips' (diarrhoea).

Our Bostons are taking off but five are attacked and shot down. One was a ball of fire and landed near our aerodrome. Quite a few of us ran towards it but the flames were too fierce for us to do anything. What a tragic experience, all we saw were three burnt bodies in the front of what had been the aircraft. It will stay with me for a long time.

SATURDAY 18TH OCTOBER

Another panic, first Junkers 87s attack, bombs coming down like hailstones, then Messerschmitt 109s flying low and strafing anything they can, but they soon scarper when the ack-ack opens up. The coloured tracers from enemy aircraft, never seem to damage anything at all. Sometimes ME109 pilots even throw hand grenades from the cockpit, hoping to hit something, but it's just a waste of time and effort. I sit tight, nice and comfortable in my little slit trench all the while.

THURSDAY 23RD OCTOBER

The enemy's paying us an early visit, 6.30am, trying to catch us out, strafing and bombing. The Stukas and ME109s are trying their best to demoralise us. It's a good job I got out of my camp bed and laid on the floor because a big piece of shrapnel has shot right through my bivouac. Thank God I did the right thing! Rommel must be desperate to break through our lines but has had no success.

A JU88 (above) shot down in the desert and a group of FW190s left behind by retreating German forces (below).

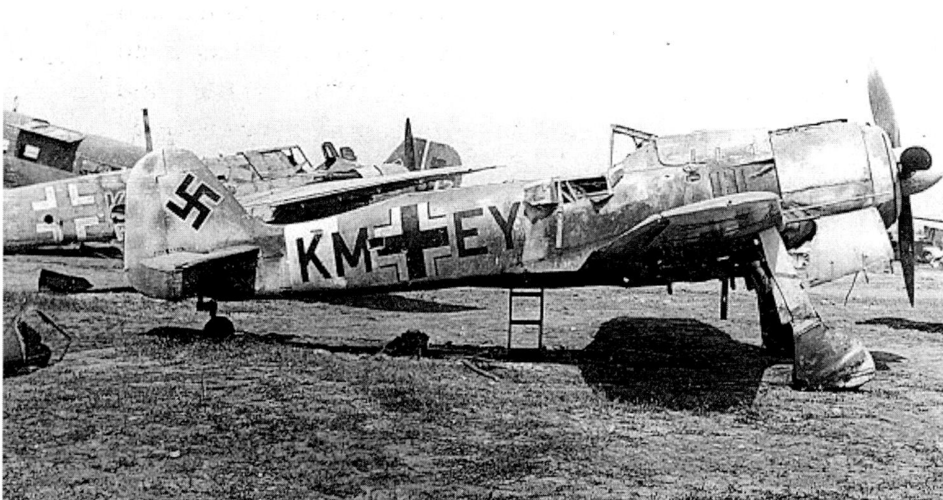

At 10 o'clock the sky lights up with every gun imaginable. All hell's let loose. We have been told the 'this is it', Montgomery has started to go all out to push back Rommel's forces. I've never heard so much noise, and believe me it's very frightening, not knowing if I'll live or die.

There is a lot of activity, tanks passing our aerodrome, armoured cars, lorries, all in one big hurry. All our aircraft just took off, and you can hear other squadrons around and about, taking to the skies. Our aircraft, having been away an hour, have just returned to be re-armed straight away, ready for combat. Pilots say that anything they see they blast at. We have been on the go for almost 12 hours, never stopping.

TUESDAY 3RD NOVEMBER

Our advance has really started, 213, 238 and 33 Squadrons have strafed enemy bases, aerodromes, aircraft, lorries and artillery; and No.1 South African Squadron has been strafing shipping, from El Alamein to Mersa Matruh, and has sunk three torpedo boats. We certainly have damaged Rommel's forces.

WEDNESDAY 4TH NOVEMBER

We are moving to an advanced aerodrome, LG172, since the Germans are retreating on all fronts and sectors. Arrived early morning at El-Daba for a two-day stay. What a horrible sight: 87 Jerry aircraft left behind and bodies all over the place, some with no legs or arms, some no heads.

No, you're not seeing things! A Heinkel III (above) and a Junkers JU87 'Stuka' (below) marked with RAF roundels and in service during the Desert War. The Stuka is being flown by P/O G.R.S. McKay. It was found by 213 Sqn at Martuba, Libya in 1942.

We were told to dig our own new trenches and not to try and use the Germans ones, they are probably booby trapped. Slept on back of lorry.

THURSDAY 5TH NOVEMBER

We have never moved so quickly, we are on our way to El-Daba. I've counted, on our journey, 250 ammunition vehicles, every one full of explosives. At some places enemy aircraft had no time to take off, some were burnt out. Papers of all kinds, maps, etc. still burning. Precautions have to be taken in case land mines have been placed around any object. Very little sleep on back of lorry.

FRIDAY 6TH NOVEMBER

Arrived at LG105, El-Daba. It's littered with military equipment, letters, photographs of German pilots' families, it seems a great pity, we are all human and to kill each other makes me feel ashamed of what I am. To murder people, what are these politicians thinking about, why don't they fight it out themselves?

SUNDAY 8TH NOVEMBER

Some horrible sights again, more bodies scattered far and wide. We have counted 63 aircraft: Junkers JU87s, Dornier D017s, Heinkel HEIIIs, Messerschmitt BF109s, Messerschmitt BF110s. We are now at LG102, Sida Nish, sleeping with our clothes on in case of emergency, because

German tanks abandoned in the desert, found at LG105 El-Daba.
The author poses with one of them (above).

the Germans don't even get a chance to settle down. We certainly have them on the run. Three days and on our way to El-Adem.

SATURDAY 14TH NOVEMBER

Moving on to Sidi Barani, through Halfaya Pass, it twists and turns, now we are climbing Sollum Pass, lots of bends, looking down it's quite a long drop, it's a very high part of Cyrenaica. Travelling past Capuzzo, where the German cemetery is, on to Bardia, Bar-El-Baheira, making inland to Gambut which we are climbing again. The road is hard sand with empty barrels to show the way the Army advance party made sure that land mines were cleared for our trucks. Stayed here for four days. Again on the move to El-Adem; not a blade of grass or even a bird, just small dried shrubs.

WEDNESDAY 18TH NOVEMBER

Travelling very slowly because of lorries carrying German prisoners going to POW camp south at Sidi Barani. The dirty Germans spat at our convoy. Left Gambut for El-Adem, arriving at 7.30; what a sight, vehicles of all kinds, armoured cars, tanks from a Panzer division, about 60 lorries, 40 tanks, about 40 aircraft, scattered all over the place. Here come the enemy Stukas with their screamers, dropping bombs, thank God our Hurricanes are up there to chase them, no damage done. The Sappers are clearing up German dead to bury somewhere. I'm still wearing battle dress and boots, also overcoat, still very cold at

Two photos of Rommel, "The Desert Fox" – inspecting the troops when in sight of Alexandria (above) and toasting a victory that never was with Afrika Corps troops (below)
Both pictures found in the desert after the German retreat.

night and hot during the day. We are restricted to one gallon of water a week for drinking and washing. I have a five-gallon German can I empty my dirty water into so that I can have a rub down when we stop now and again. Here comes a BF109 strafing all over the place, but the Army flak shoots him clean out of the sky. God rest the pilot's soul.

SUNDAY 29TH NOVEMBER

On our way to Martuba, LG2, detoured Tobruk because Germans are trying to bomb the harbour to stop our reinforcements, but our flak seems to drive them off. Anyway, we have arrived at Martuba LG2 after all that excitement at 7.30. Had a meal of spuds, corned dog, peas, rice pudding and tea.

I put up my bivouac and dig a trench big enough to get my camp bed into and about a foot to spare, so that I can get in and out of bed and that's where I'm going right now. I wonder if I will live another day. There are tanks, vehicles, aircraft, motor bikes, which Jerry didn't have time to take, scattered all over the place and bodies too. The army red cross are taking care of them. Next day two mates and I walk along the cliff tops and see a horrible sight – four bodies, no arms or legs. We follow a path which leads into a cave and find it is full of rifles, there must be hundreds. Explosives and hand grenades too. We don't go in, it's almost certain to be booby trapped. We visit Derna, but there is very little there, just a few Italians walking around the streets. Glad to be back in camp. We

Italian soldiers surrender to the Durham Light Infantry at Mersa Matruh, Egypt.

The end of their war: defeated Afrika Corps soldiers are led away to POW camps.

stay at Martuba for a while, almost 34 days. On the move tomorrow.

SATURDAY 4TH JANUARY, 1943

On the move at 5 o'clock in the morning, fully clothed, overcoats and boots on. Passing El-Hania, Tokra, Benghazi, on to Agedabia, Marsa Brega, El-Ghelia. We are the advanced fighter squadron. German aircraft are still trying to bomb our convoy and the only airfield to operate will be Crete. It's still a frightening experience, maybe we will live another day. Germans and Italians have 110 aerodromes in North Africa, but still use Sicily and Greece for long distance bombers and fighters. We stop at aerodromes on the way to re-arm our aircraft because the enemy use landing grounds at Tunis and Tripoli.

WEDNESDAY 8TH JANUARY

Proceed to Sirte, sleep near the famous Marble Arch, a monument to Mussolini, the Italian President. We moved next day on our journey through the Arch and on to our destination, Misurata, Tripolitania.

THURSDAY 9TH JANUARY

Arrived at our destination, Misurata, we now have driven the enemy out of Tunis and Tripoli. Bedding down for the night, what a change from being uneasy. Peaceful, not a gun or enemy anywhere. Looking on to the road we can see telegraph wires, with camel bodies hanging from them;

Dernah. The tragic consequences of war. The graves of two RAF pilots, buried by the Germans (above) and a German cemetary (below).

they must have hit land mines. Also two Arabs lying in a pitiful sight, dead.

We stay here for quite a while from January until 6th July when we move back to Idku, in Egypt. The war here is finished, thank God! All that way and I'm still alive, no more sweating and fear. It's really been a nightmare, thinking of dying every day. I think we are all exhausted, all those miles from Misurata back to Idku, fortunately a peaceful journey, all that track on the back of a lorry.

Our Squadron is split up, we are equipped with Spitfires. 'B' Flight is sent back to Larnaca, Cyprus; 'A' Flight is to remain at Idku.

PART FOUR

Back to Cyprus

FEBRUARY 25TH, 1943

No action at all on Cyprus, just seems like peace time. We are in Nissen huts for a change but still keep our aircraft ready, because some parts of Greece are occupied by the Germans and their aircraft now and again appear, but are soon chased off by our squadron. The Turks and Cypriots are still at each other's throats, there's a curfew in Nicosia. We have been issued with Mustang IIIs, equipped with Browning guns and long range tanks for reconnaissance and strafing and bombing islands like Rhodes, Dodecanese, Naxos and Crete, with resounding success and without any losses. I find them very easy to re-arm and load with bombs. Pilots say that Crete now has very few enemy aircraft and no ack-ack at all. There are rumours that we are moving to Brindisi, it seems all of our equipment, lorries, etc are to be moved to the docks in Larnaca for an emergency move.

We fly to Brindisi in a Douglas DC3 (Dakota), another frightening experience with no parachutes, passing Crete, Greece, up to Brindisi, Italy. What a relief when we touch down on *terra firma*, the Germans still have one or two airfields in Greece, but fortunately for us their stocks of petrol are running out. We stay at Brindisi to re-arm and bomb up, ready for a raid on Corfu, just off Greece, to strafe anything they see matter what the objects are. When the operation is finished our aircraft are to go over Corfu to Toffia, near Brindisi. We are moving to operate from there. Stayed four days, then moved up to Camerino where our accommodation is in Nissen huts. Our landing strip was a short journey from camp, can't grumble about the food, very good. We are here until 10th February, 1945, then we move to Zadar, Yugoslavia.

An RAF Mustang IV in the Balkan Air Force, 1944.

We receive new Mustang IVs with modern armament, etc. I stay for two months, where a few of us finished our term overseas and are now on our way home. We fly to Naples, stay a fortnight, are taken to Rome for a week's holiday and see the Vatican City and all the important places, then return back to Naples. A week after that we set sail for home, past Sardinia, down towards the Straits of Gibraltar, again a frightening experience going into the Atlantic Ocean, hearing those blasted waves bashing up against the side of the ship. We are down on the bottom decks again. Passed Spain, France, Channel Islands. There are no German U-boats to worry about but we are thinking of stray mines.

But thank God, who has decided to spare my life! We arrive at Liverpool docks on the 15th of May, 1945, VE Day!

Addendum

On 16th February, 1944, F.O. Gordon Steinberg's Hurricane (DR 563) was shot up and he had to bale out over the Mediterranean. He was rescued by a 'friendly' destroyer but died of his injuries; he had completed 92 sorties, flying over Cyprus, the Mediterranean and the Western Desert.

Flying Officer Steinberg has no known grave but his name is inscribed on the Alamein War Memorial in Egypt. He was a real 'character' and had a way all his own; he would not put up with red tape and official nonsense, like the incident over his painting the Star of David on the nose of his aircraft...

This hadn't been officially sanctioned and even when remonstrated with by the Wing Commander, the Squadron Leader and the Adjutant of 213 Squadron, he wouldn't back down and remove the emblem. He told them what he thought of them and eventually, when they realised that they were going to get nowhere with him, they walked away, muttering: "What's the use!"

NOMINAL ROLL 213 SQUADRON

11th MAY, 1941

PILOTS

Squadron Leader MacDONALD (DFC)

'A' Flight	*'B' Flight*
F/Lt. GOULD	F/Lt. LOCKHART
F/O TEMLETT (DFC)	P/O WESTLAKE (DFC)
F/O SOWERY	P/O DOWNIE
P/O BRIGGS	P/O LYNCH
P/O PAIN	P/O CROWTHER
P/O DOWTHWAITE	P/O POUND
Sgt. P. A. WILSON	Sgt. F. A. WILSON
Sgt. MARSHALL	Sgt. WALLACE
Sgt. SISSON	Sgt. HANCOCK (DFC)
Sgt. EDWARDS	Sgt. WHITE (DFM)
Sgt. Simms	Sgt. GLEDHILL
Sgt. BOYD	Sgt. HENDERSON

F/Lt. G. H. WESTLAKE - 18th SEPT., 1942 (DFC)
P/O A. J. HANCOCK - 28th July, 1942 (DFC)
F/O A. U. HOULE - 4th Dec., 1942 (DFC)
Sq. Ldr. R. P. OLIVER - 5th Jan., 1943 (DFC)

NOMINAL ROLL 213 SQUADRON

1st JUNE. 1942

PILOTS

Squadron Leader M. A. YOUNG (DFC)

'A' Flight

F/Lt. C. A. TEMLETT (DFC)
F/O J. A. SOWREY
F/O J. L. BRIGGS
P/O P. P. WILSON
P/O W. H. THOMLINSON
F/Sgt. W. R. HENDERSON
F/Sgt. K. N. R. SISSONS
F/Sgt. L. O. H. BOUCHER
F/Sgt. J. AVISE
F/Sgt. STEPHENSON
F/Sgt. H. M. COMPTON
Sgt. J. D. RITCHIE
Sgt. H. A. AITKEN
Sgt. JACKSON
Sgt. HEWICK
Sgt. R. W. JONES
Sgt. G. S. BOLTON

'B' Flight

F/Lt. G. A. WESTLAKE
F/O J. C. EDMUNDS
P/O F. A. W. J. WILSON
P/O g. J. HANCOCK
P/O G. R. S. MacKAY
P/O W. N . SWINDON
P/O D. REHILL
P/O C. D. A. SMITH
W/O R. J. WALLACE
F/Sgt. W. A. LACK
F/Sgt. J. EDWARD
F/Sgt. F. H. HALVORSEN
Sgt. J. F. C. BALLANTYNE

SOME OF THE SHIPS IN THE CONVOY ESCORT

HMS HOOD (Battleship)
HMS EXETER (Destroyer)
HMS KOSIC (Destroyer)
HMS ZULU (Destroyer)
HMS ARGUS (Aircraft Carrier)
HMS FURIOUS (Aircraft Carrier)

CONVOY

GEORGIC (Troopship) - I was on this.
ARRANDER
DUCHESS OF BEDFORD
FLYING DUCHESS
WINDSOR CASTLE
STRATHMORE *
STRATHEDEN *

My diary must conclude by thanking our transport drivers Palmer, Kit Thomson and John Hutchinson, who risked their lives to bring fresh supplies of ammunition and spare parts. Below they are bringing a new airscrew (propellor) for a Hurricane from Heliopolis to our base at Idku (1942).

213 Squadron Armoury section, Cyprus 1942 (above) and at El Adem, Nov 22, 1942 (below).